Alan Bradley

The Other Face of the Cross
The Forbidden Testament of Death on Calvary
by Barnabas

Original Title: *The Other Face of the Cross*
Copyright © 2022 by Alan Bradley
All rights reserved to Booklas.com
This book is intended for personal and spiritual development. The information and practices described here are based on studies, traditional knowledge, and the experiences of authors and specialists in this field. This content does not replace medical advice or conventional therapies, serving only as a complementary resource for personal well-being and growth.

Editor
Luiz Antonio dos Santos

Proofreading
Mariana Sousa
Carlos Almeida
Ana Ribeiro

Graphic Design and Layout
Juliana Costa

Cover
Renato Fernandes

CIP-BRASIL. CATALOGING-IN-PUBLICATION DATA
The Other Face of the Cross / Alan Bradley.
Booklas, 2024.
Apocryphal texts. 2. Gospels. 3. Biblical studies. I. Sousa, Mariana. II. Title.
09-3652
DDC 229
UDC 27-58

All rights reserved by
Editora Booklas
Rua José Delalíbera, 962
86.183-550 – Cambé – PR
Email: suporte@booklas.com
www.booklas.com

Sumário

Prologue 5
Chapter 1 Who Was Barnabas 7
Chapter 2 Relationship with Christ 12
Chapter 3 Humble Origins and Spiritual Formation 17
Chapter 4 Meeting Paul 22
Chapter 5 Missionary Journeys 27
Chapter 6 Parting Ways 32
Chapter 7 Controversial Legacy and the Apocryphal Gospel 38
Chapter 8 Content of the Apocryphal Gospel 43
Chapter 9 Different Perspectives 49
Chapter 10 Lasting Influence 55
Chapter 11 Martyr of Faith 61
Chapter 12 Friend of God 66
Chapter 13 Defender of Unity in the Early Church 71
Chapter 14 Mentor of Leaders 76
Chapter 15 Diplomat of Faith 81
Chapter 16 Exemplary Virtues 86
Chapter 17 Persecution and Exile 91
Chapter 18 Tireless Evangelist 96
Chapter 19 Inspired Writer 101
Chapter 20 Oral Tradition and Spiritual Legacy 106
Chapter 21 Disciple of Jesus 111
Chapter 22 Leadership in the Church 116
Chapter 23 Theology and Doctrine 121
Chapter 24 Inclusive and Ecumenical Vision 126

Chapter 25 Relics and Traditions 131
Chapter 26 Cultural Influence 136
Chapter 27 Patron of Artists 141
Chapter 28 Accounts of Miracles and Healings 146
Chapter 29 Charisma and Spiritual Power 151
Chapter 30 Intellectual Legacy 156
Chapter 31 Artistic Representation 161
Chapter 32 Veneration and Popular Worship 166
Chapter 33 Ecumenical Relations 171
Chapter 34 Expansion of Christianity 176
Chapter 35 Historical Controversies 181
Chapter 36 Manuscripts and Historical Documents 186
Chapter 37 Legends and Popular Narratives 191
Chapter 38 Patron of Specific Causes 196
Chapter 39 Interpretations During the Reformation and Counter-Reformation 201
Chapter 40 Archaeological Discoveries 206
Chapter 41 Ecological Dimension and Spirituality 211
Chapter 42 Academic Studies and Modern Research 216
Chapter 43 Contemporary Relevance 222
Chapter 44 Interfaith Dialogue 227
Chapter 45 Popular Devotion Worldwide 233
Chapter 46 Educational Legacy 238
Chapter 47 Final Reflection - The Eternal Legacy of Barnabas 244
Epilogue 249

Prologue

As you open this book, you come face to face with a revelation that history has attempted, in vain, to bury. This text carries a forbidden secret, concealed for centuries in the shadows of collective memory and hidden manuscripts—a secret that suggests one of the greatest controversies of early Christianity: the crucifixion of Jesus.

This rediscovered manuscript bears immense weight, an alternative gospel that challenges the very pillars of Christianity as we know it. The **Gospel of Barnabas** emerges from the depths of obscurity as a long-lost testament to events on Golgotha that few have dared to consider. In this gospel, Barnabas, a companion of Paul and witness to the early persecutions of Christians, unveils a shocking narrative: Judas Iscariot—the betrayer, the disciple—was the one crucified in place of Jesus. To the eyes of orthodoxy, this account becomes a dangerous and inconceivable heresy. But why suppress this version? Why would Barnabas, a fellow believer, be disavowed by religious leaders?

The answers may lie in the very history of this manuscript. Found in an abandoned monastery in the remote mountains of Damascus, the Gospel of Barnabas resurfaced from the ruins—a text forgotten from a time when doctrines were being shaped and dissenting voices silenced. It was rediscovered in fragments and transcripts, carefully preserved by monks who, over centuries, recognized the power of this forbidden gospel. The authenticity of these fragments, confirmed by scholars and paleographers, revealed a chronology and style tracing back to the early centuries following the death of Christ. Scientific analyses of the pigments, fibers, and inscriptions date it to a time when eyewitnesses still shared living memories of the events surrounding Christ.

As scholars unraveled its lines, they found elements that challenge the official narrative and broaden the scope for interpretation. In the Gospel of Barnabas, there is a clear rejection of Jesus' divinity and a detailed description of the crucifixion that questions the foundations of Christianity. And as these fragments were discovered and translated, a story began to emerge, told from the eyes of one who lived and breathed the impact of Christ and His disciples' words and deeds. Barnabas—whose name means "son of encouragement"—shares in this gospel a perspective that both consoles and challenges, offering an alternative narrative: that Jesus, as a true prophet, was spared from the fate reserved for traitors and sinners. He was saved by divine intervention, while Judas—the one who betrayed Him—was placed on the cross in His stead, mistaken by the crowd as the Messiah.

But what makes this version plausible? How do we discern history from myth? The authenticity of the documents suggests they were preserved with great care, and contemporary scientific methods allow us to trace the origins of their materials and language, confirming they date to a time when Barnabas was still a living memory in Christian tradition. Additionally, its contents echo certain oral traditions that circulated among early Christian sects and were later suppressed as institutional Christianity took hold. For many, this gospel represents a missing piece, a fragment of truth concealed beneath centuries of reinterpreted dogmas and traditions.

Thus, in reading these pages, you are not merely unveiling a forbidden account—you are approaching one of the oldest and most controversial witnesses to the life of Christ. The words of Barnabas, forgotten and ignored, have finally been brought to light, inviting you to a profound and provocative understanding of what truly took place during that fateful crucifixion. Between the lines lies the voice of a man who witnessed the formation of Christianity's earliest steps, a voice that asks to be heard once again, challenging the reader to reevaluate what they believe to be true.

Chapter 1
Who Was Barnabas

The figure of Barnabas emerges from the pages of the New Testament as a beacon of faith, charity, and unwavering dedication to the message of Christ. His name itself—meaning "son of encouragement"—seems almost prophetic, reflecting the role he would play among the early followers of Christianity. As one of the earliest disciples, Barnabas occupies a unique position within Christian history, bridging cultural divides and working to strengthen the bonds of the nascent Church. Yet, despite the profound impact he had, Barnabas remains, to many, an enigmatic figure whose story is often overshadowed by the apostles with whom he worked so closely.

Barnabas first appears in the Book of Acts, a historical account of the early Church attributed to Luke, one of the evangelists. This text provides the foundational details of Barnabas's life, painting a portrait of a man whose commitment to the Christian faith was as deep as it was transformative. Acts describes him as a Levite from Cyprus, suggesting a background steeped in Jewish tradition and religious observance. Yet, unlike many of his contemporaries who might have been reluctant to embrace the teachings of Christ, Barnabas's heart was open to the profound shift that the Christian message represented. His actions and choices reveal a man who was deeply invested in the unity, growth, and survival of the fledgling Christian community.

Barnabas's introduction to the early Christian community is marked by an act of profound generosity. In Acts 4:36-37, we learn that he sold a field he owned, bringing the money to the apostles and laying it at their feet as an offering. This act was not merely a gesture of charity but a sign of his complete devotion to the cause. Barnabas's gift likely provided essential support for the community, meeting the practical needs of the apostles and other early disciples. This act also suggests a renunciation of worldly attachments—a theme that would recur throughout his life as he devoted himself to the work of spreading the Gospel.

But who was Barnabas beyond his acts of generosity? His very name, a title given by the apostles, hints at the role he played within the early Christian community. To be called the "son of encouragement" speaks to a person of compassion, empathy, and the ability to inspire others. Barnabas's character was indeed central to his ministry; he encouraged believers, supported fellow missionaries, and was known for his unwavering faith and kindness.

The New Testament presents Barnabas as a man of great spiritual power and wisdom. Although not one of the twelve apostles chosen by Jesus, Barnabas nonetheless occupies a revered position within the early Church. He is considered an "apostle" in a broader sense, a term used in Acts 14:14, acknowledging his status as one sent to spread the Gospel. This distinction places him among those early leaders who had authority within the Church, respected by fellow disciples and followers for his insight and dedication. Indeed, his reputation as a spiritual leader is highlighted when the apostles in Jerusalem send him to Antioch to examine reports of a new, vibrant Christian community.

In Antioch, Barnabas encounters a diverse group of believers—Jews and Gentiles alike, worshiping together. Instead of viewing the Gentile converts with suspicion or demanding strict adherence to Jewish customs, Barnabas recognizes the grace of God at work among them. His reaction is not to impose restrictions but to encourage and nurture their faith. Acts 11:23 describes how he rejoiced and exhorted them all to remain steadfast in their commitment to Christ, underscoring his role as an encourager and unifier within the Church. This approach reflects a forward-thinking, inclusive vision of Christianity that would later become a defining characteristic of the faith. His time in Antioch would also set the stage for one of the most pivotal relationships of his ministry—that with Saul, later known as Paul.

When Saul arrives in Antioch, it is Barnabas who welcomes him, bridging the gap between this new convert and the established community of believers. Saul's past as a persecutor of Christians made many wary of him, yet Barnabas saw beyond Saul's former life, recognizing the transformative power of his faith and his potential as a leader. By vouching for Saul, Barnabas enabled his integration into the Christian community, providing him with a platform to share his insights and eventually become one of the faith's most influential figures.

The relationship between Barnabas and Paul is essential to understanding Barnabas's role in the early Church. Together, they embarked on missionary journeys, spreading the Gospel to distant lands, establishing new Christian communities, and enduring hardships along the way. Yet, even in this partnership, Barnabas's humility stands out. Although Paul would eventually become more prominent within the Church, Barnabas remained steadfast in his support, demonstrating a willingness to work alongside others rather than seeking personal glory. His humility and dedication to the mission exemplify the qualities that made him a pillar of the early Christian community.

Barnabas's inclusion of Gentiles into the Christian faith also speaks to his expansive vision of the Gospel. Unlike some who saw Christianity as an extension of Judaism, bound by its customs and laws, Barnabas embraced a broader perspective. He recognized that the message of Christ transcended cultural and religious boundaries, offering salvation to all who believed. This understanding would later place him at the center of one of the early Church's most significant debates—the inclusion of Gentile believers and the extent to which they were expected to adhere to Jewish customs.

This tension came to a head at the Council of Jerusalem, where Barnabas once again played a crucial role. The council convened to address the question of whether Gentile converts needed to follow Jewish laws, such as circumcision, to be considered part of the Christian community. Barnabas, along with Paul, argued for the freedom of Gentile believers from these requirements, advocating for an inclusive approach that welcomed all into the fold without the burden of additional ritual obligations. Their stance was eventually upheld, marking a turning point in the Church's development and establishing Christianity as a faith that transcended traditional ethnic and cultural boundaries.

In this way, Barnabas's life and ministry encapsulate the spirit of the early Church—a movement rooted in compassion, inclusion, and unwavering faith. His commitment to fostering unity among believers, his courage in the face of adversity, and his humility in service reveal a man wholly devoted to the teachings of Christ. Through his actions, Barnabas demonstrated that faith was not merely a matter of belief but one of practice, lived out in service to others and in the pursuit of justice and unity.

Yet, even with his undeniable impact, Barnabas's story in the New Testament is surprisingly limited in scope. Much of what we know about him comes from the Book of Acts, with a few additional mentions in Paul's letters. This scarcity of information has led to a certain mystique surrounding his life, fueling speculation and inspiring apocryphal works that sought to fill in the gaps. One such text, the Gospel of Barnabas, would later emerge, purportedly offering insight into his teachings and beliefs. While this text is widely considered non-canonical and controversial, it nonetheless reflects the enduring fascination with Barnabas and his legacy.

In examining the life of Barnabas, we are reminded of the importance of those early followers who, though perhaps less well-known, were instrumental in the foundation and spread of Christianity. Barnabas's role as an encourager, a unifier, and a servant-leader underscores the diversity of gifts within the body of believers. His life serves as a testament to the power of faith and the profound impact that one dedicated individual can have on the world.

Barnabas's story is thus one of quiet strength, an unassuming yet profound dedication that helped shape the course of Christian history. Through him, we glimpse a faith that is not only personal but deeply communal, one that reaches across boundaries to embrace all who seek the light of Christ. His legacy, though often overshadowed, remains a vital part of the Christian narrative—a reminder of the enduring power of encouragement, humility, and the courage to embrace a vision of faith that transcends division.

Chapter 2
Relationship with Christ

The name Barnabas reverberates through early Christianity with an aura of simplicity, loyalty, and an unswerving sense of purpose. Yet, at the heart of his journey lies a profound relationship with Christ—a bond that defined his mission and shaped his understanding of faith, devotion, and sacrifice. For Barnabas, Jesus Christ was more than a teacher or a distant figure of divinity; He was the center of an emerging path, one that Barnabas embraced with unwavering conviction. This relationship is less about documented interactions with Jesus Himself, as Barnabas does not feature among the twelve apostles, and more about his deep spiritual alignment with the teachings, compassion, and transformative essence of Christ. His faith was neither fragile nor hesitant; it grew from a solid foundation that embraced both the awe of the divine and the struggles of humanity.

The first glimpses of Barnabas's affinity for Christ arise in his actions and values. In Acts, where Barnabas appears as a generous supporter of the early Christian community, his actions echo the message of Jesus: a commitment to selflessness, compassion, and the relinquishing of earthly possessions for a greater cause. By selling his land and laying the proceeds at the apostles' feet, Barnabas performs an act of total surrender, mirroring Christ's own sacrifice for humankind. In the tradition of Christ's teachings, Barnabas gives of himself to uplift others, demonstrating that true devotion is an act of giving rather than receiving.

Barnabas's understanding of Jesus's message went far beyond theological understanding; it was a lived experience, embodied in his approach to his ministry. His relationship with Christ was characterized by a faith that could cross boundaries, welcoming Gentiles and Jews alike into the nascent Christian fold. It is evident that Barnabas saw Jesus as a universal Savior, and he aligned himself with a mission that transcended the divisions of his time. In his travels and interactions, Barnabas's actions reveal his acceptance of Jesus as the Messiah for all, a notion that would eventually challenge prevailing beliefs and bring him into theological debates, particularly around the inclusion of non-Jewish converts. Barnabas was not deterred by this; his loyalty to the spirit of Jesus's ministry—a ministry of acceptance and compassion—was far more significant to him than traditional religious boundaries.

This relationship with Christ becomes even more evident when we consider Barnabas's stance during critical moments in the life of the early Church. The new Christian movement was often marked by internal struggles, particularly regarding the integration of Gentile converts. Barnabas's firm position in favor of inclusion shows his commitment to what he believed was Jesus's vision of a faith that welcomed everyone, regardless of background or tradition. He stood by Paul in the debate over circumcision, defending the rights of Gentile converts to practice the faith without adopting all Jewish customs. His actions speak to a deeply spiritual bond with Christ, one that prioritized the message of love, unity, and transformation over rigid ritual or cultural divisions.

Barnabas's acceptance of Jesus as the Messiah did not merely manifest in his role as an advocate but also in the depth of his compassion. In this, he reflected Christ's own empathy and boundless kindness, a quality that distinguished Jesus's ministry. Barnabas was known for his role as the "son of encouragement," an epithet that resonates with Jesus's message of hope and healing. When others faltered, Barnabas stepped in to uplift, to reassure, to encourage—and, most notably, he did so with a sense of gentleness that reflected the essence of Jesus's teachings. His ability to see potential in others, especially in those overlooked by society, mirrored Jesus's approach to His followers. This was not mere kindness; it was the embodiment of Christ-like love, a testament to how deeply Barnabas internalized Jesus's example.

Perhaps the most striking example of Barnabas's connection with Jesus lies in his relationship with Saul, who would later become Paul. Saul, a former persecutor of Christians, was treated with caution and suspicion by many within the early Church. Yet Barnabas, recognizing Saul's transformative encounter with Jesus, took him under his wing, trusting in the power of Christ's redemption. In doing so, Barnabas followed in the footsteps of Jesus, who often saw beyond outward appearances to the heart and soul of individuals. His acceptance of Saul was not a simple matter of forgiveness; it was a profound act of faith in the power of Jesus's love to change lives. Barnabas became Saul's advocate, standing by him when others hesitated. This act of trust and acceptance allowed Saul to step into his role as Paul, one of Christianity's greatest apostles. Barnabas, in essence, enabled Paul's journey, seeing in him the potential to contribute greatly to the mission of spreading the Gospel. This moment encapsulates the depth of Barnabas's faith in Christ—a faith that trusted in the potential for transformation, that believed in the redemption of every soul touched by Jesus's message.

Barnabas's perspective on the Messiah also extended to his views on leadership and discipleship. Where others might have sought recognition or authority, Barnabas's dedication to Christ was evident in his humility. He served not for personal gain but for the glory of God, always redirecting attention to Jesus's teachings rather than his own accomplishments. This was a lesson Barnabas seemed to understand intimately: that the true path of discipleship lay in self-forgetfulness and in uplifting others. He accepted his role not as a leader for the sake of status but as a steward of Jesus's legacy, a servant to his fellow believers. His humility, like his compassion, was another manifestation of his bond with Christ, and it became one of the defining traits of his ministry.

Though we have no record of Barnabas directly meeting Jesus, the connection he shared with Christ was rooted in something profound—a conviction that went beyond mere belief and bordered on an experiential understanding of Jesus's mission. His actions spoke of someone who knew, at the very core of his being, that he was following in the footsteps of the Divine. He walked the same path of sacrifice, endured the same hardships, and shared the same message of hope. This bond with Jesus is apparent in every decision he made, in the way he encouraged others, in the way he mediated conflicts, and in the way he served as a bridge between differing factions. It was a relationship grounded in a shared purpose and an unyielding commitment to the Gospel.

As Barnabas embarked on missionary journeys with Paul, his relationship with Christ continued to shape his every step. They ventured into hostile territories, facing opposition and danger, yet Barnabas's faith never wavered. He remained committed to spreading the message of Jesus, regardless of the challenges. This resilience, this ability to endure persecution and hardship, is another testament to the depth of his connection with Christ. It was not a connection of convenience but one of complete surrender to the path that Jesus had set before him. His relationship with Christ was one that demanded everything of him—his comfort, his safety, his possessions, and even his personal desires. And Barnabas gave freely, without hesitation, because he understood the value of the calling he had received.

The strength of Barnabas's relationship with Christ is perhaps best illustrated in the way he lived out Jesus's teachings through action rather than words alone. In his ministry, Barnabas was not merely a preacher but a doer, one who exemplified the core tenets of Christianity through his life. He embraced the stranger, he welcomed the outcast, he encouraged the faint-hearted, and he stood firm in the face of opposition. His life was his testimony, a living reflection of the message of love, forgiveness, and hope that Jesus had shared with the world. Barnabas did not just speak of Christ; he embodied Christ's teachings in a way that drew others to the faith. He was, in every sense, a disciple—not because he had known Jesus personally, but because he had taken the teachings of Jesus to heart and let them transform every aspect of his life.

Barnabas's legacy within the Church and his contributions to Christian thought continue to echo this relationship with Christ, revealing a faith that was as personal as it was universal. His story reminds us that the depth of one's connection to Christ is not solely measured by proximity to the historical Jesus but by the extent to which one's life aligns with His teachings. Barnabas's commitment to compassion, unity, and humility was not just a reflection of his faith; it was a reflection of the Christ he followed so devoutly. Through Barnabas, we see the enduring power of Jesus's message, a message that transcended time and culture, bringing people together in a bond that went beyond earthly affiliations.

In every sense, Barnabas was a servant of Christ, an emissary of the love that Jesus had shown to the world. He carried forth the message of redemption, not with grandiosity, but with a simplicity that spoke of a heart fully surrendered to God. His journey reveals that a true relationship with Christ is not about status, recognition, or even miracles; it is about walking in love, in humility, and in the quiet power of faith. Barnabas's legacy stands as a reminder that the path of discipleship is one of courage, of selflessness, and of a deep, abiding commitment to the teachings of Christ. Through his life, he invites us to reflect on our own journey, on the ways in which we, too, might embody the values of compassion, unity, and faith. His story, though interwoven with the struggles and triumphs of the early Church, ultimately points us back to Christ, urging us to see in him the path toward a deeper, more meaningful relationship with the Divine.

Chapter 3
Humble Origins and Spiritual Formation

In the warm sun of Cyprus, amidst the salt-scented breeze and rugged hills, Barnabas was born into a life that would shape his understanding of faith, community, and service. The land was a crossroads of cultures and traditions, a melting pot where Greek, Roman, and Jewish influences mingled, bringing with them an array of beliefs and practices. Growing up here, Barnabas's worldview was undoubtedly influenced by this diversity, by a landscape that embraced both the ancient traditions of Israel and the emerging Greco-Roman influences. This fusion of worlds would mold him into a man capable of bridging divides, a trait that would define his role in the early Christian Church.

Barnabas's roots trace back to the tribe of Levi, one of the ancient tribes of Israel traditionally dedicated to religious service in the Temple. As a Levite, Barnabas was likely raised with a keen sense of his religious heritage, steeped in the sacred traditions and rituals of his people. Yet his birth and upbringing in Cyprus placed him on the outer fringes of Jewish society, in a community of Diaspora Jews, far from the central influence of Jerusalem. This background gave Barnabas a dual perspective; he was, by birth and blood, part of the Jewish faith, yet by residence and upbringing, part of a more cosmopolitan, Hellenistic world. This dual identity would come to serve him well, allowing him to navigate the different cultures he encountered in his ministry with ease and understanding.

From an early age, Barnabas's life would have been imbued with the spiritual practices of Judaism. He would have learned the Torah, recited the Shema, and observed the rituals and customs that marked Jewish life. The Jewish community in Cyprus, like other Diaspora communities, was one of solidarity and resilience, united by a shared heritage and a faith that had sustained them through generations of displacement. In this environment, young Barnabas would have developed a sense of identity rooted in both his Jewish heritage and the larger, diverse world around him. This unique upbringing nurtured in him a profound respect for tradition alongside an openness to the wider world—a combination that would later allow him to embrace Christianity's expansive vision.

In the eyes of his community, Barnabas likely stood out from an early age. His generosity, compassion, and wisdom, qualities that would later define his ministry, may have been recognized and nurtured by those around him. It is likely that Barnabas's family instilled in him values of humility, kindness, and dedication to God—qualities revered within Jewish culture and essential for anyone considering a life of spiritual service. While little is known about his family's specific circumstances, it is possible that they were people of modest means, grounded in their faith and dedicated to the well-being of their community. Such a background would have fostered in Barnabas a sense of humility, an understanding of life's hardships, and a commitment to serve others—all of which would be crucial in his later mission.

For Barnabas, the choice to follow the path of Christ marked a profound spiritual transformation, yet it was not a departure from his faith but rather a fulfillment of it. His understanding of Jesus as the Messiah was deeply rooted in his knowledge of the Hebrew Scriptures and the promises they contained. As a Levite, Barnabas would have been well-versed in the prophecies and sacred texts that spoke of a coming redeemer, one who would bring salvation to Israel and unite the nations under God's reign. When he encountered the message of Christ, he recognized it not as a rejection of his heritage but as the culmination of it. In this sense, Barnabas's faith journey was not one of renunciation but of deepened understanding, an evolution that harmonized his Jewish identity with his Christian mission.

It is worth contemplating the decision Barnabas made when he chose to leave behind his previous life and embrace the Gospel. In a world where familial ties, social structures, and religious identity were deeply intertwined, such a decision would have carried immense consequences. To follow Christ was to step into a new identity, one that redefined his relationships, his goals, and his very purpose. By embracing Christianity, Barnabas was not only taking on a new faith but also committing himself to a life of itinerant ministry, poverty, and persecution. Yet, it is this choice that reveals the strength of his spiritual formation—the depth of his conviction that Jesus was indeed the awaited Messiah, and that his mission was to spread this truth, no matter the cost.

Barnabas's generosity, as depicted in Acts when he sold his field and gave the proceeds to the apostles, is one of the clearest indications of his humble spirit and willingness to surrender earthly wealth. Such an act would not have been easy, for land in that era represented stability, legacy, and identity. In choosing to give it away, Barnabas was aligning himself with Christ's teachings on humility and detachment, embracing the path of a true disciple. This act of selflessness was not isolated but rather indicative of a larger pattern in his life—a willingness to put the needs of others before his own and to relinquish worldly attachments in favor of spiritual devotion. For Barnabas, the renunciation of material possessions was an outward sign of an inward transformation, a testament to his commitment to the way of Christ.

His spiritual formation is further evidenced by his unrelenting pursuit of unity within the Christian community. Barnabas was a man who recognized the value of peace and reconciliation, striving to bring people together rather than allow divisions to take root. He understood that the path of discipleship required humility—not only the humility to serve others but also the humility to accept differences, to be patient, and to build bridges between people of different backgrounds. This was no small feat in a community that was grappling with profound questions about identity, tradition, and the inclusion of Gentiles. Yet Barnabas's humble origins, his understanding of life outside the strict boundaries of Jerusalem, equipped him to navigate these challenges with grace. His role as a mediator, as one who could speak to both Jewish and Gentile believers, was invaluable to the early Church's cohesion and growth.

The humble beginnings of Barnabas also instilled in him a deep empathy for others, especially for those marginalized or overlooked. His compassion extended to all he encountered, whether they were newly converted believers or former persecutors like Saul. This empathy was not a surface trait but a profound characteristic of his faith, shaped by his experiences and by a spirituality that valued people over power, relationships over rituals. In this, Barnabas embodied a core aspect of Jesus's teachings, living out a love that transcended societal boundaries. His upbringing in a diverse cultural setting likely reinforced this perspective, allowing him to see each person as a child of God, worthy of respect and dignity.

As he embarked on his missionary journeys, Barnabas carried with him the lessons of his early years—the resilience, humility, and empathy that had defined his formation. His message was one of hope and inclusion, a Gospel that invited all to the table, Jew and Gentile alike. He did not preach a faith confined by the walls of Jerusalem or the limits of tradition; instead, he proclaimed a message that reached out to the world, grounded in his own experience of God's boundless love. His life serves as a reminder that spiritual formation is not a single moment but a continuous journey, one that begins with humble origins and grows through each choice, sacrifice, and act of compassion.

Barnabas's story, though often overlooked, is one of profound transformation, shaped by the spiritual principles he learned in his youth. He was a man who understood the value of humility, not as a weakness but as a strength that allowed him to serve without seeking glory. His life stands as a testament to the idea that true discipleship is not measured by status or power but by the willingness to serve, to forgive, and to embrace a path of selflessness. In his unwavering commitment to the teachings of Christ, Barnabas reveals that humility and faith are intertwined, that a life rooted in God is one that seeks not personal gain but the greater good.

Through the example of Barnabas, we see that spiritual formation is not merely a matter of knowledge or tradition; it is a lived reality, a journey marked by acts of kindness, sacrifices, and a continual return to God's call. His origins may have been humble, but his spirit was vast, encompassing a love and dedication that would inspire generations to come. As we look back on his life, we are reminded that the path to true greatness is found not in accolades or wealth but in the quiet strength of a servant's heart. It is this legacy, born from his humble origins, that makes Barnabas a pillar of faith—a model of humility, resilience, and unwavering devotion to the Gospel.

Chapter 4
Meeting Paul

Barnabas's life took a pivotal turn when he encountered Saul of Tarsus, a man whose transformation from persecutor to apostle remains one of the most powerful narratives in Christian history. This meeting was not merely a chance encounter, nor was it a relationship marked by convenience. It was a partnership divinely orchestrated, one that would shape the course of early Christianity, blending the strength of Barnabas's compassionate heart with the fiery conviction of Saul, later known as Paul. Together, they would embark on missionary journeys that would break new ground and open doors to regions and people far beyond the borders of Judea. Yet, their alliance was not without struggle, requiring both men to reconcile differences and cultivate a mutual respect that would ultimately define their mission.

When Saul converted to Christianity after his dramatic encounter on the road to Damascus, he was left isolated, mistrusted by many in the early Christian community. Saul's reputation as a fervent persecutor of Christians had preceded him, and it was understandably difficult for many believers to accept that he had genuinely changed. His former zealotry had caused suffering and fear within the fledgling Church, making his sudden conversion a source of skepticism. It was at this critical juncture that Barnabas emerged as a bridge, a figure willing to look beyond Saul's past and welcome him with open arms. Barnabas's decision to extend trust and friendship to Saul would mark the beginning of a partnership that would have a profound impact on the Christian mission.

Barnabas's willingness to embrace Saul as a brother speaks to his innate empathy and spiritual insight. Where others saw only the persecutor, Barnabas saw the potential for redemption. He saw the calling that God had placed on Saul's life and recognized the authenticity of his conversion. In this, Barnabas was living out the teachings of Christ, who had instructed His followers to forgive, to love one's enemies, and to believe in the transformative power of faith. Barnabas did not merely offer Saul a second chance; he offered him a place within the community, vouching for him and helping him establish credibility among the apostles. By doing so, Barnabas demonstrated a rare courage, a willingness to stand beside the outcast and proclaim, "This one, too, is my brother."

This meeting, which took place in Jerusalem, is documented in Acts 9:26-27, where Barnabas brings Saul before the apostles, introducing him and recounting his conversion story. This act of advocacy was no small gesture; it was a public declaration of support, one that required Barnabas to place his own reputation on the line. He spoke on Saul's behalf, testifying to the sincerity of his conversion and his commitment to Christ. In doing so, Barnabas became Saul's gateway into the Christian community, a role that would allow Saul to become Paul, the great apostle to the Gentiles. Barnabas's support was not merely a kindness; it was the catalyst that enabled Paul's mission, his letters, and his profound impact on Christian theology.

After this initial meeting, Saul returned to Tarsus for a time, while Barnabas continued his work in the early Church. However, it wasn't long before their paths crossed again. When a growing Christian community emerged in Antioch, Barnabas was sent by the apostles to observe and support this new congregation, which included a significant number of Gentile converts. Seeing the potential for growth in this diverse community, Barnabas sought out Saul, bringing him to Antioch to help nurture and teach the new believers. This decision illustrates Barnabas's humility and his keen insight into the needs of the Church. Rather than attempting to lead alone, Barnabas recognized Saul's unique gifts and invited him to share in the work, creating a partnership that would become one of the most effective alliances in the history of Christian missions.

Antioch became a pivotal center for the early Christian movement, and it was here that the followers of Christ were first called "Christians." Barnabas and Saul spent a year in Antioch, teaching and building up the community. Their collaboration here was a seamless blending of Barnabas's gentle guidance and Paul's intellectual rigor, combining the pastoral care of Barnabas with the doctrinal depth of Paul. Together, they shaped a community that was diverse, inclusive, and deeply committed to the teachings of Jesus. The Church in Antioch would soon become a launching point for their missionary journeys, serving as a model for the inclusive vision of Christianity that would later spread across the Roman Empire.

As they set out from Antioch on their first missionary journey, Barnabas and Paul ventured into uncharted territories, bringing the Gospel to places where the message of Christ had not yet reached. They traveled through Cyprus, Barnabas's homeland, where they preached to both Jews and Gentiles, bridging the cultural and religious divides that had previously separated these communities. Barnabas's familiarity with the region and its people undoubtedly played a role in their success, allowing them to connect with the local populace on a personal level. His presence lent credibility and warmth to their mission, endearing them to those they encountered.

Throughout their travels, Barnabas and Paul encountered a mix of reception and resistance. Their message was radical, challenging the religious norms and social structures of the time. They faced opposition from both Jewish and Roman authorities, as well as from local leaders who felt threatened by the growth of this new faith. Yet, the bond between Barnabas and Paul helped them endure these challenges. They encouraged one another, supported each other in times of hardship, and shared in the triumphs and tribulations of their mission. Their partnership was not merely practical; it was a testament to the power of friendship, faith, and a shared commitment to spreading the Gospel.

One of the defining moments of their journey occurred in Lystra, where they performed a miracle, healing a man who had been crippled from birth. The local people, astonished by the miracle, attempted to worship Barnabas and Paul as gods, calling Barnabas "Zeus" and Paul "Hermes." This incident, recorded in Acts 14, illustrates the depth of misunderstanding that often accompanied their mission. While the miracle demonstrated the power of the Gospel, the people's reaction underscored the cultural and spiritual gap that Barnabas and Paul sought to bridge. In response, they rejected the worship of the crowd, directing them instead to the true God. This moment exemplifies the humility and integrity of both men, who consistently redirected glory away from themselves and toward God.

However, the partnership between Barnabas and Paul was not without tension. Their journey together revealed not only their strengths but also their differences, which would later lead to a painful but defining split. The most significant source of friction came with the involvement of John Mark, a young disciple who accompanied them on their missionary travels. At a certain point, John Mark left the mission, and when he later wished to rejoin, Paul refused, deeming him unreliable. Barnabas, however, wanted to give John Mark another chance, reflecting his characteristic compassion and belief in redemption. This disagreement would ultimately lead to a separation between Barnabas and Paul, marking the end of their direct collaboration but also paving the way for new paths in their respective missions.

Despite their parting, the influence of Barnabas on Paul's life and ministry remained profound. It was Barnabas who had first introduced Paul to the apostles, who had vouched for his sincerity, and who had worked alongside him to build the Church in Antioch. Their partnership had brought the Gospel to places it had never been heard, establishing communities of faith that would continue to grow and flourish. Even in their differences,

Barnabas and Paul shared a deep respect for one another, bound by the shared mission that had defined their time together.

The legacy of their partnership is a reminder of the strength found in unity, even amid conflict and divergence. Barnabas and Paul, though distinct in personality and approach, complemented each other in ways that amplified their impact. Barnabas's empathetic heart softened Paul's fiery zeal, while Paul's intellectual rigor sharpened Barnabas's gentle approach. Together, they modeled a vision of Christian community that was inclusive, courageous, and willing to engage the world around them with compassion and conviction.

Through his relationship with Paul, Barnabas demonstrated that true discipleship requires more than personal faith; it demands a willingness to stand beside others, to offer guidance and forgiveness, and to trust in God's power to transform lives. His faith in Paul, his support during difficult times, and his decision to advocate for reconciliation all reflect the depth of his commitment to Christ's teachings. This partnership was not only a strategic alliance but a spiritual brotherhood, forged in the fires of shared mission and tempered by the trials they faced together.

Barnabas's meeting with Paul, then, was far more than a chance encounter; it was the meeting of two souls driven by a common vision, each bringing to the other strengths that would shape the Church's mission for generations to come. Their story reminds us that the path of faith is not one we walk alone but one we share with others, even when that path leads to challenging conversations, disagreements, or farewells. Barnabas's unwavering support of Paul reflects a love that transcends differences—a love that, in the end, speaks to the very heart of the Gospel they both preached. Through their partnership, we see the transformative power of friendship in ministry, a power that continues to inspire and guide believers across time.

Chapter 5
Missionary Journeys

The journeys that Barnabas and Paul embarked upon are among the most compelling chapters in the story of early Christianity. Their travels stretched across cities and regions, carrying the Gospel into places that had never heard of Jesus Christ. Together, they endured the rigors of ancient travel, encountered resistance and persecution, and inspired diverse communities with a message of hope, salvation, and unity. Barnabas, with his humble and inclusive spirit, was not only Paul's companion but an equal partner, helping shape the mission of the early Church. Each journey was more than a mere geographical expedition; it was a pilgrimage of faith, a testament to the courage, resilience, and profound conviction that characterized both men.

The account of Barnabas and Paul's first missionary journey begins in Antioch, a thriving city with a vibrant Christian community. Antioch had become a hub for believers from various cultural backgrounds, embodying the inclusivity that would come to define the early Church. Here, Barnabas and Paul were set apart for their mission by the Holy Spirit, an act that underscored the divine calling on their lives. The community, led by prayer and fasting, laid hands on them, sending them forth as emissaries of the faith. This ceremonial beginning marked not only the start of their travels but also the Church's commitment to spreading the Gospel beyond the boundaries of Judea.

Their first destination was the island of Cyprus, Barnabas's homeland. The choice of Cyprus was significant, as

Barnabas's familiarity with the people and culture of the island provided them with a welcoming foundation for their mission. They traveled through the cities of Salamis and Paphos, preaching in synagogues and speaking to anyone who would listen. This first leg of the journey reflected Barnabas's approach to evangelism—beginning with those who shared his background and traditions, extending an invitation to the new faith while respecting their shared heritage.

In Paphos, Barnabas and Paul encountered their first major challenge: the opposition of a Jewish sorcerer and false prophet named Elymas. Elymas sought to undermine their message and dissuade the Roman proconsul, Sergius Paulus, from accepting the Gospel. Paul, filled with the Holy Spirit, rebuked Elymas, causing him to be struck blind. This powerful demonstration of divine authority not only silenced Elymas but also convinced the proconsul of the truth of their message. The incident underscored the spiritual authority that both Paul and Barnabas carried, a force that was not to be trifled with. Through this act, they asserted that the message of Christ was not merely a philosophy but a divine truth, one that could withstand and overcome opposition.

From Cyprus, they traveled to the mainland, arriving in the region of Pisidia. Here, they encountered mixed reactions to their message, as their teachings spread through both Jewish and Gentile communities. Their time in Antioch of Pisidia would be a defining moment, as it was here that they first experienced serious opposition from Jewish leaders who rejected their teachings. In response, Paul and Barnabas declared that they would turn their attention to the Gentiles, a decision that marked a pivotal shift in their mission. This moment was not a rejection of Judaism but a recognition that the message of Christ was meant for all people, transcending cultural and religious boundaries. Barnabas, with his inclusive vision, readily embraced this new focus, understanding that the Gospel was a message of unity, calling all people to God's grace.

Their journey continued through Iconium, Lystra, and Derbe, cities where they faced both enthusiastic acceptance and fierce opposition. In Iconium, they initially found success, preaching to both Jews and Greeks. However, their success soon attracted the ire of local authorities, and they were forced to flee when a plot to stone them was discovered. In each city, they encountered people of various backgrounds, each bringing their own beliefs, questions, and doubts. Barnabas, with his empathetic nature, approached these communities not with condemnation but with an open heart, seeking to understand their lives and offer them the hope of the Gospel.

In Lystra, Barnabas and Paul experienced a unique and unexpected reaction. After performing a miracle by healing a man who had been crippled from birth, the locals mistakenly believed that the two men were gods in human form. Barnabas was identified as Zeus, and Paul as Hermes, a misunderstanding that reflected the depth of the cultural divide they faced. The people of Lystra began to offer sacrifices to them, prompting Barnabas and Paul to tear their garments and urgently insist that they were mere men, messengers of the living God. This incident highlighted the challenges of cross-cultural evangelism; even as they sought to share the message of Christ, they had to bridge the gap of misunderstanding, patiently guiding people away from their former beliefs and toward the truth of the Gospel.

Despite these challenges, Barnabas and Paul persevered, preaching boldly and establishing small communities of believers in each place they visited. Their journey was not without risk; in Lystra, Paul was stoned and left for dead by a hostile crowd. Yet, even in the face of such violent opposition, he rose up and continued his mission, demonstrating the resilience and courage that defined both him and Barnabas. This unwavering commitment to their calling reveals the depth of their faith, a conviction that could not be shaken by threats, persecution, or physical harm.

The journey of Barnabas and Paul was not merely about winning converts but about establishing communities rooted in faith, love, and mutual support. They appointed elders in each city, ensuring that the new believers had spiritual leaders who could guide them in their absence. This act of establishing leadership within each community underscores Barnabas's and Paul's understanding of the Church as a living body, one that needed structure and care to thrive. They did not simply preach and move on; they invested in the growth and stability of each congregation, ensuring that the seeds they planted would continue to bear fruit long after they had moved on.

As they traveled, Barnabas and Paul faced not only external opposition but also internal tensions. The presence of John Mark, who had accompanied them initially but left partway through the journey, became a point of contention between the two. Barnabas, ever compassionate, saw potential in John Mark and wished to offer him another chance, while Paul, with his uncompromising nature, felt that John Mark's departure indicated unreliability. This difference in perspective would later lead to their eventual separation, yet it also highlights the distinct qualities each man brought to their mission. Barnabas's inclination to mentor and forgive reflects his nurturing spirit, a characteristic that shaped his approach to leadership and ministry.

Upon returning to Antioch, Barnabas and Paul shared the stories of their journey, recounting the miracles, challenges, and triumphs they had experienced. They spoke of the Gentiles who had come to faith, the communities they had established, and the lives that had been transformed. Their testimony was a source of encouragement for the believers in Antioch, reaffirming the power and reach of the Gospel. It was clear that their mission was bearing fruit, that the message of Christ was spreading far beyond the borders of Judea, and that the seeds they had planted were growing into strong, vibrant communities of faith.

The legacy of Barnabas and Paul's missionary journeys cannot be overstated. They pioneered a vision of Christianity that embraced all people, breaking down barriers and challenging the cultural norms of their time. Their journeys laid the foundation for a global faith, one that would reach beyond the confines of a single region or ethnicity. Through their partnership, they demonstrated that the Gospel was not bound by tradition or geography; it was a universal message, one that could find a home in every heart open to its truth.

For Barnabas, these journeys were the culmination of his deepest beliefs—a faith that saw no division between Jew and Gentile, a love that reached across boundaries, and a commitment to serve others without seeking recognition or reward. His partnership with Paul, though marked by differences and eventual separation, remains a testament to the power of unity in mission. Together, they faced dangers, endured hardships, and brought the light of Christ to places that had known only darkness.

Through their missionary journeys, Barnabas exemplified the qualities of a true disciple—humility, courage, and an unwavering commitment to God's calling. His actions were a living testament to the message he preached, embodying the compassion, grace, and strength that defined the early Church. His story serves as a reminder that the journey of faith is not always easy, that it often requires sacrifice, resilience, and a willingness to face the unknown. Yet, in walking this path, Barnabas not only fulfilled his mission but also inspired countless others to do the same.

The journeys of Barnabas and Paul continue to inspire, reminding us that faith is a journey, one that takes us beyond the familiar and into the unknown. Their story speaks of a love that crosses boundaries, a courage that endures trials, and a hope that transcends all understanding. Through Barnabas, we see a man whose faith was not confined to words or beliefs but was lived out in action, in service, and in a life wholly dedicated to the mission of Christ.

Chapter 6
Parting Ways

The friendship between Barnabas and Paul, once so united in purpose and vision, eventually reached a crossroads that would lead to one of the most poignant separations in early Christian history. Their parting was not one of enemies but of two deeply committed men whose convictions and approaches to ministry had grown apart over time. Though they had faced countless dangers and challenges together, spreading the Gospel across cities and regions, this moment marked a turning point in their partnership—a divergence shaped by differing perspectives, tempered by personal loyalties, and ultimately forged in the crucible of faith.

The source of their division lay in a disagreement over a young man named John Mark, a relative of Barnabas and a disciple who had accompanied them during the initial stages of their first missionary journey. However, partway through the journey, John Mark chose to leave and return to Jerusalem, an action that Paul interpreted as an abandonment of their mission. To Paul, this decision reflected a lack of resolve, a sign of unreliability that could compromise their work. For Barnabas, however, John Mark's departure did not signal weakness or disloyalty; instead, he saw a young man who might have stumbled but was deserving of another chance. To Barnabas, nurturing and guiding John Mark was a way to extend the grace and patience that were central to his own understanding of discipleship.

This difference in perspective between Barnabas and Paul, though seemingly focused on a single person, reflected a deeper divide in their approaches to ministry. Paul, driven by an intense sense of purpose and urgency, believed that their mission demanded unwavering commitment, a strength that would not waver in the face of adversity. Barnabas, in contrast, viewed discipleship as a journey, one that allowed for growth, failure, and redemption. His natural inclination was to encourage and support those who struggled, seeing potential where others might see inadequacy. This compassionate approach was the essence of his ministry—a willingness to meet people where they were and to walk with them toward growth and transformation.

As the time came for their second missionary journey, Paul and Barnabas found themselves at an impasse. Barnabas, still hopeful and trusting, wanted to bring John Mark along once more, believing that he deserved a chance to prove his commitment. Paul, however, was adamantly opposed, unwilling to risk another disruption in their mission. Acts 15:39 describes their disagreement as so "sharp" that they decided to part ways. It was a decision neither took lightly, but one that ultimately reflected the depth of their convictions. Their parting was not born of bitterness but of an unyielding dedication to what each man believed was best for the mission they had been called to fulfill.

This separation, though painful, was perhaps inevitable. Barnabas and Paul were both strong-willed, passionate individuals, united by faith but distinct in their approaches. Their divergence, while regrettable, underscored the diversity within the early Church—a movement that, even in its infancy, held a range of perspectives, personalities, and methods for spreading the Gospel. Barnabas, who had once introduced Paul to the apostles and vouched for his sincerity, now found himself on a different path, one that would lead him to new territories and new disciples.

After parting from Paul, Barnabas took John Mark with him and set sail for Cyprus, his homeland. This choice was not merely logistical but symbolic, representing Barnabas's commitment to nurturing young believers and providing them with opportunities to grow. By bringing John Mark along, Barnabas demonstrated a faith in people that mirrored the patience and forgiveness Christ had extended to His own disciples. In choosing to guide John Mark, Barnabas was upholding the very values that had defined his ministry from the beginning—a spirit of encouragement, a belief in redemption, and a commitment to seeing potential where others saw failure.

The journey to Cyprus marked a new chapter in Barnabas's ministry, one that emphasized his role as a mentor and spiritual guide. In returning to familiar ground, Barnabas may have found comfort in the landscape of his youth, a place that had shaped him and nurtured his own faith. Here, he would continue his mission with the same dedication and humility that had characterized his work alongside Paul. His separation from Paul did not diminish his zeal or his commitment to spreading the Gospel; if anything, it reaffirmed his unique calling to support and uplift those who might otherwise be overlooked.

Paul, for his part, chose Silas as his new companion, embarking on a journey that would take him through Syria and Cilicia, strengthening the churches they had established and continuing the mission they had begun together. Though their paths had diverged, both Paul and Barnabas remained true to the calling they shared, albeit in different ways. Paul's ministry, marked by letters and teachings that would profoundly shape Christian theology, continued to expand and evolve, reaching new cities and bringing the message of Christ to an ever-widening audience. His relentless drive and intellectual rigor would make him one of the most influential figures in Christian history, his work laying the foundations for much of Christian doctrine and practice.

The story of Barnabas and Paul's parting offers a lesson in the complexities of human relationships within the context of faith. Their separation was not a failure but a reflection of the diversity within the early Church. It reveals that unity does not always mean uniformity, that there is room within the faith for different approaches, methods, and perspectives. Barnabas's compassion and Paul's discipline were not opposites but complements, each contributing to the mission in its own way. Their separation allowed each man to pursue his vision of ministry more fully, leading to a broader spread of the Gospel and the establishment of stronger, more resilient Christian communities.

Although we do not have extensive records of Barnabas's activities following his separation from Paul, tradition holds that he continued his work with undiminished fervor. His legacy as a mentor is perhaps best reflected in the life of John Mark, who would later go on to become a significant figure in the early Church. Many scholars believe that John Mark is the author of the Gospel of Mark, one of the four canonical Gospels, a text that would serve as a cornerstone of Christian teaching and inspiration for centuries. Barnabas's willingness to give John Mark a second chance, to invest in his potential, ultimately bore fruit in ways that he himself may never have foreseen. Through John Mark, Barnabas's legacy endured, a testament to the power of grace, patience, and encouragement.

The impact of Barnabas and Paul's separation extended beyond their own lives, shaping the development of the Church itself. Their differing approaches illustrated the need for diversity within the body of believers, showing that the message of Christ could be carried forth through various voices, each bringing a unique perspective and strength. This diversity would become one of Christianity's greatest assets, allowing it to adapt, grow, and reach people from all walks of life. The early Church, though often divided by geography, culture, and interpretation, was united by a shared faith in Christ—a unity that transcended individual disagreements and forged a path forward, even in the face of conflict.

The parting of Barnabas and Paul is also a reminder that God's purposes are often fulfilled in unexpected ways. What may appear as a setback or division can, in the hands of the Divine, become a means of expansion and growth. Through their separation, both Barnabas and Paul were able to pursue new opportunities, reaching communities that might otherwise have remained untouched. Their individual journeys, though distinct, were both integral to the spread of the Gospel and the establishment of the Church.

As we reflect on the story of Barnabas and Paul, we are reminded that faith is a journey marked by both companionship and individuality. There are moments when we walk side by side with others, sharing in the joys and challenges of the path. And there are moments when we must forge our own way, trusting in the calling that has been placed upon us. For Barnabas, this meant stepping away from a treasured friendship, accepting that his mission would lead him down a different path. It was a choice made not in anger or resentment, but in faith, a recognition that the work of God could continue even in the face of separation.

In the end, the legacy of Barnabas and Paul is one of resilience, adaptability, and grace. Their parting did not weaken their mission; rather, it allowed each to fulfill his calling in a way that was true to his own gifts and vision. Barnabas's role as a mentor, encourager, and servant of Christ continued to shine, illuminating a path for those who sought a second chance, who needed guidance, and who longed for a compassionate hand. Paul's role as a theologian, teacher, and relentless apostle of the Gospel would transform the Christian faith, providing it with a theological foundation that endures to this day.

Through their parting, Barnabas and Paul left a legacy that speaks to the heart of the Christian journey—a journey that encompasses both unity and diversity, both collaboration and independence. Their story is a testament to the idea that even in separation, there can be growth, and even in disagreement, there can be respect. Barnabas's choice to nurture John Mark, and Paul's determination to press forward, reflect two sides of a faith that is both forgiving and disciplined, compassionate and resolute. Their lives remind us that faith is not a monolithic experience; it is a tapestry woven from the unique contributions of each individual, each path, and each moment of courage.

In parting ways, Barnabas and Paul allowed their faith to flourish in new directions, carrying forth a Gospel that was as diverse as the people it sought to reach. Their story continues to inspire, a reminder that the path of discipleship is one of both togetherness and solitude, one that calls us to walk with others yet remain true to our own calling. Through Barnabas, we see the power of grace and encouragement; through Paul, we see the strength of conviction and determination. Together, they left a legacy that echoes through the ages, a legacy that reminds us that in the end, all roads of faith lead to the same Divine purpose.

Chapter 7
Controversial Legacy and the Apocryphal Gospel

As time passed, Barnabas's legacy took on dimensions both complex and controversial. While he was revered within the early Christian community as a figure of compassion and encouragement, the centuries that followed would see his name associated with mystery, intrigue, and a controversial text that claimed to bear his teachings: the Gospel of Barnabas. This apocryphal gospel—an account that exists outside the accepted canon—would go on to raise questions and spark debates, not only about Barnabas himself but also about the theological and cultural currents that shaped early Christianity. Its content, historical context, and later interpretations have created a lasting enigma surrounding Barnabas, intertwining his legacy with issues of authenticity, doctrine, and identity.

The early Christian tradition holds Barnabas in high regard, celebrating him as a dedicated apostle, a mentor, and a bridge-builder among diverse communities. In the Book of Acts and in Paul's letters, Barnabas is depicted as a man of unwavering faith, committed to spreading the Gospel and nurturing new believers. Yet, over time, as the early Church struggled to define its identity and doctrines, various texts surfaced that claimed to hold hidden or alternative teachings of Jesus and his disciples. Among these was the so-called Gospel of Barnabas, a work that emerged much later than the accepted New Testament writings and diverged significantly from the canonical Gospels.

The origins of the Gospel of Barnabas are shrouded in mystery, with the text's earliest surviving manuscripts dating back only to the medieval period—specifically, to the 14th and 15th centuries. Despite its title, this text was almost certainly not written by Barnabas himself. Scholars widely agree that the gospel is anachronistic, containing details, language, and theological concepts more aligned with medieval Islamic thought than with the world of first-century Christianity. The text presents a portrayal of Jesus and his teachings that is inconsistent with the canonical Gospels and reflects influences from both Islamic and Christian sources, leading most scholars to regard it as a product of interfaith dialogues or polemics of a much later era.

This apocryphal gospel diverges sharply from the New Testament narratives, particularly in its portrayal of Jesus and its theological claims. One of the most striking features of the Gospel of Barnabas is its denial of the crucifixion, a core event in Christian theology. According to this text, Jesus was not crucified; instead, it claims that Judas Iscariot was miraculously substituted in his place, a narrative that aligns more closely with certain Islamic interpretations of Jesus than with traditional Christian doctrine. Additionally, the text explicitly denies the divinity of Christ, presenting him solely as a prophet and teacher rather than as the Son of God. This portrayal of Jesus and the denial of the crucifixion have led scholars to conclude that the Gospel of Barnabas may have been written to support a theological perspective that aligned with Islamic beliefs, potentially as a means of fostering dialogue or as a polemical response to Christian doctrines.

The authorship and motivation behind the Gospel of Barnabas remain subjects of speculation. Some scholars suggest that it was written by a Christian convert to Islam or by someone with knowledge of both faiths, intending to bridge the theological divide or offer an alternative narrative. The historical context of the text's appearance—the period of medieval Europe, when Islam and Christianity were frequently in contact through trade, scholarship, and conflict—suggests that it may have been created as a work of interfaith discourse. Its content reflects elements familiar to Islamic audiences, possibly as an attempt to present a version of Jesus's life and teachings that would resonate within an Islamic framework.

The name "Barnabas" itself likely served as a strategic choice by the text's unknown author. Barnabas, known in Christian tradition as a close companion of Paul and a figure of humility and grace, carried an authority that would lend credibility to the work. By attributing the gospel to Barnabas, the author could appeal to both Christian and Muslim readers, suggesting an authentic link to an early apostle. The use of Barnabas's name implied a continuity of tradition, as though this text preserved teachings or insights that had been overlooked or suppressed by the mainstream Church. However, despite its title, there is no evidence to suggest that Barnabas himself had any role in the creation of this gospel, nor that it accurately reflects his views or teachings.

For many centuries, the Gospel of Barnabas remained relatively obscure, known only in limited circles and surviving in a few manuscript copies. However, in the modern era, particularly in the 20th century, the text resurfaced and attracted renewed attention, often within the context of interfaith debates. Some Islamic scholars have cited the Gospel of Barnabas as evidence that early Christian teachings were more compatible with Islamic views than with established Christian doctrines. In this sense, the text has been used by some as a means of validating Islamic perspectives on Jesus, suggesting that the canonical Gospels had been altered or misinterpreted over time. However, mainstream Christian scholarship rejects the Gospel of Barnabas as a historically unreliable document, emphasizing its late authorship and inconsistencies with both early Christian and Islamic sources.

The legacy of the Gospel of Barnabas is thus a complex one, entangled in issues of religious identity, historical interpretation, and the quest for authenticity. For some, it represents an alternative narrative that challenges traditional Christian beliefs; for others, it is a spurious text with no legitimate connection to early Christianity. The debates surrounding it reflect broader questions about the nature of scripture, the transmission of religious teachings, and the ways in which different faiths interpret and revere the figure of Jesus.

While the Gospel of Barnabas may bear his name, it does not align with the character and mission of the Barnabas depicted in the New Testament. Barnabas, as portrayed in Acts, was a man deeply committed to the teachings of Christ as conveyed by the apostles—a believer in the divinity of Jesus, the redemptive power of His crucifixion, and the unity of the early Church. His dedication to spreading the Gospel alongside Paul, his defense of Gentile inclusion, and his role as a mentor to John Mark all suggest a man who fully embraced the core doctrines of early Christianity. The message attributed to him in the apocryphal gospel, by contrast, is incompatible with the beliefs he upheld in his lifetime.

Despite this, the existence of the Gospel of Barnabas has added a layer of mystique to Barnabas's legacy, shaping perceptions of him in ways that extend beyond the historical record. This association illustrates the powerful influence that names and narratives can wield in shaping religious history, as well as the ways in which figures from the past are sometimes reimagined to fit the theological or ideological needs of later generations. Barnabas, who spent his life promoting unity, compassion, and understanding, might have been dismayed to see his name associated with a text that fuels division and controversy. Yet, in a way, his legacy continues to bring people together, even if in unexpected and contentious ways.

The Gospel of Barnabas also underscores the importance of discernment in the preservation and interpretation of religious texts. The early Church took great care in discerning which writings authentically reflected the teachings of Jesus and the apostles, a process that led to the formation of the New Testament canon. Texts like the Gospel of Barnabas, though intriguing, fall outside the boundaries of this carefully curated collection, serving instead as reminders of the diverse interpretations and perspectives that existed—and continue to exist—within the larger story of Christianity.

In the broader context of Barnabas's legacy, the Gospel of Barnabas is a curious footnote rather than a defining feature. The true legacy of Barnabas lies in his life, his actions, and his dedication to the early Church. He was a man of courage and compassion, a bridge between cultures, and a mentor who believed in the redemptive power of grace. His story, as preserved in the New Testament, remains a powerful testament to the transformative power of faith and the importance of encouragement and unity in the Christian journey.

Through the controversies surrounding the Gospel of Barnabas, the enduring relevance of Barnabas's life becomes even more apparent. His example continues to inspire believers to seek truth with humility, to embrace others with compassion, and to remain steadfast in faith. In a world where differing interpretations and ideologies often lead to division, Barnabas's legacy reminds us of the strength found in unity, the value of patience, and the importance of a faith grounded in love and service.

Ultimately, the apocryphal gospel that bears his name does not diminish the genuine contributions of Barnabas to early Christianity. Instead, it serves as a reminder of the enduring complexities of religious history and the ways in which the past can be interpreted, reinterpreted, and sometimes misappropriated. For those who seek to understand Barnabas, his true legacy lies not in apocryphal texts but in the canonical accounts of his life—a legacy of encouragement, humility, and an unshakable commitment to the Gospel of Christ. Through this lens, Barnabas remains a steadfast pillar of the early Church, his life a beacon of faith that continues to shine through the centuries, unclouded by the shadows of controversy.

Chapter 8
Content of the Apocryphal Gospel

The Gospel of Barnabas, despite its disputed origins and questionable authenticity, has continued to captivate readers with its unique and provocative content. This apocryphal text, which claims to recount teachings and events from the life of Jesus, diverges markedly from the canonical Gospels and introduces theological perspectives that have sparked intrigue and controversy over the centuries. Although widely dismissed by scholars as a work of later origin, likely from the medieval period, the Gospel of Barnabas offers insights into the religious and cultural dynamics of its time. Its contents, while not reflective of Barnabas's actual teachings or beliefs, reveal an alternate narrative of Jesus's life and mission that raises important questions about faith, interpretation, and the boundaries of orthodoxy.

The Gospel of Barnabas is structured as a series of dialogues and teachings, interwoven with stories of Jesus's life that resemble those found in the canonical Gospels. However, its portrayal of Jesus diverges sharply from the accounts of Matthew, Mark, Luke, and John. The Jesus of the Gospel of Barnabas is a prophet and teacher, revered and inspired, but not divine. In this text, Jesus consistently denies his divinity and emphasizes his role as a servant of God, explicitly identifying himself as a mere human messenger rather than the Son of God. This portrayal directly contrasts with the New Testament, where Jesus's divine nature is central to His mission and teachings. By presenting Jesus solely as a prophet, the Gospel of Barnabas aligns more closely with Islamic views than with early Christian doctrine, which holds Jesus as both fully divine and fully human.

One of the most controversial aspects of the Gospel of Barnabas is its treatment of the crucifixion. In the canonical Gospels, the crucifixion of Jesus is a pivotal event—the ultimate act of sacrifice through which redemption is offered to humankind. The Gospel of Barnabas, however, presents an entirely different narrative: it claims that Judas Iscariot was made to look like Jesus and was crucified in His place. According to this account, Jesus was taken up to heaven unharmed, while Judas's deception and betrayal resulted in his own death on the cross. This substitution theory closely resembles Islamic teachings on the crucifixion, as found in the Qur'an, which states that Jesus was not crucified but was instead raised to God. The Gospel of Barnabas thus appears to promote a narrative that aligns with Islamic beliefs, casting doubt on the crucifixion and resurrection that are foundational to Christian theology.

Another significant deviation in the Gospel of Barnabas is its portrayal of Jesus's relationship with the apostles and His teachings on salvation. In this text, Jesus frequently warns against worshipping Him or placing undue emphasis on His role, insisting instead on the sole authority and unity of God. The text emphasizes that salvation is achieved through adherence to God's commandments and the rejection of idolatry, positioning Jesus more as a moral guide than as a redeemer. In line with this interpretation, the Gospel of Barnabas downplays the concepts of original sin and atonement, central themes in Christian theology that underscore humanity's need for a Savior. Instead, it presents a form of ethical monotheism that echoes Islamic teachings on personal responsibility and obedience to God.

The Gospel of Barnabas also differs from the New Testament Gospels in its narrative style and tone. While the canonical Gospels are marked by a simplicity and brevity that reflect their focus on Jesus's teachings and actions, the Gospel of Barnabas is more expansive, often delving into lengthy dialogues that reflect philosophical and theological ideas. It includes elements that appear to respond to Christian doctrines that had developed over time, such as the Trinity, the Incarnation, and the idea of Jesus as the Son of God. By emphasizing Jesus's role as a prophet and His subservience to God, the text implicitly critiques these doctrines, positioning itself as a corrective to what it perceives as deviations from true monotheism.

The apocryphal gospel also contains unique parables and teachings that are not found in the canonical Gospels. For instance, in one passage, Jesus condemns the notion of amassing wealth and encourages His followers to live simply and to dedicate themselves wholly to the service of God. This theme resonates with the portrayal of Barnabas in Acts as a man of generosity who sold his property to support the Christian community. However, these teachings are presented in a way that aligns with the moral emphasis of Islamic thought, emphasizing piety, humility, and strict obedience to divine law. The text appears to advocate for a form of asceticism and self-discipline, underscoring a vision of spirituality that emphasizes personal purity and detachment from worldly concerns.

One of the most intriguing aspects of the Gospel of Barnabas is its explicit prediction of the coming of Muhammad. In a number of passages, the text presents Jesus as foretelling the arrival of a future prophet, who will complete the work that He Himself began. This prophet is identified by name as Muhammad, and the text positions him as the fulfillment of the divine revelation that Jesus had initiated. This prophecy, which has no parallel in the canonical Gospels, is one of the strongest indications that the text was likely intended to appeal to Muslim readers or to support Islamic views on prophecy and revelation. By positioning Muhammad as the ultimate prophet, the Gospel of Barnabas aligns itself with the teachings of Islam and presents a narrative that diverges significantly from the Christian view that Jesus is the culmination of God's revelation.

The gospel's description of Jesus's teachings is also distinctly anti-Pauline, suggesting that the author was familiar with and perhaps critical of Paul's influence on Christian doctrine. In several passages, the text implies that Jesus's true teachings were misunderstood or distorted by later followers, with specific reference to concepts such as the divinity of Christ and salvation through faith. These critiques seem directed at the theology that Paul developed in his epistles, which emphasized salvation by grace and the divinity of Christ. The Gospel of Barnabas, by contrast, advocates for a return to what it presents as the original, unaltered message of Jesus—a message that focuses on obedience to God's laws, moral integrity, and the rejection of any form of worship directed at Jesus Himself.

The Gospel of Barnabas, with its emphasis on monotheism, denial of the crucifixion, and prediction of Muhammad, has naturally raised questions about its origins and purpose. Many scholars believe that it was written in a context of interfaith dialogue, where its teachings could serve as a bridge between Christian and Islamic beliefs. Some have suggested that it was crafted by a Christian convert to Islam or by a Muslim familiar with Christian scripture, intending to offer a perspective on Jesus that aligned with Islamic theology. The text's presence in Europe during the Middle Ages, a time marked by significant interaction between Christian and Muslim scholars, further supports this hypothesis. However, no definitive evidence exists regarding the authorship or exact motivation behind its creation, leaving its origins a subject of ongoing scholarly inquiry and speculation.

Despite its lack of historical authenticity, the Gospel of Barnabas has been embraced by some as a legitimate alternative account of Jesus's life, particularly within certain Muslim communities. For these readers, the text offers a portrayal of Jesus that aligns with Islamic teachings and presents a version of early Christianity that feels familiar and accessible. This perspective has led to a renewed interest in the Gospel of Barnabas in the modern era, with translations and studies of the text appearing in various languages and scholarly contexts. However, mainstream Christian scholarship rejects the text as a reliable source, emphasizing its late authorship and theological inconsistencies with early Christian teachings.

The influence of the Gospel of Barnabas highlights the complexities of religious identity and interpretation, particularly in the context of Christianity and Islam. Its narrative reflects an attempt to reconcile Jesus's life and message with an Islamic worldview, suggesting a theological continuity that bridges the two faiths. Yet, in doing so, it departs from the historical and theological foundations of early Christianity, presenting a Jesus who is fundamentally different from the figure revered by Christians as the Son of God and Redeemer. The text thus occupies a unique space within religious literature—a work that, while lacking historical credibility, speaks to the enduring desire for understanding, dialogue, and connection between two of the world's major religions.

Ultimately, the content of the Gospel of Barnabas serves as a reminder of the diverse interpretations and perspectives that have surrounded Jesus's life and teachings. While the canonical Gospels remain the authoritative sources for Christians, the existence of texts like the Gospel of Barnabas reveals the range of ways in which Jesus has been understood and venerated across different cultures and belief systems. This apocryphal gospel, with its distinct theological emphasis, invites reflection on the broader questions of faith, scripture, and the boundaries of orthodoxy.

For Barnabas himself, as known through the New Testament, this apocryphal text does not represent his beliefs or teachings. The true Barnabas was a man of encouragement and faith, deeply devoted to the Christian message of salvation through Jesus Christ. His life was a testament to the inclusivity, unity, and grace that defined the early Church, and his teachings aligned with the core doctrines of Christianity. The Gospel of Barnabas, while bearing his name, ultimately stands apart from his legacy, offering an alternative narrative that reflects the theological and cultural currents of a later era.

In the context of Barnabas's life and mission, the apocryphal gospel remains a curiosity, a testament to the ways in which religious figures and narratives can be reimagined to serve diverse purposes. Yet the true legacy of Barnabas lives on in the canonical scriptures and the early Christian communities he helped establish—a legacy of encouragement, dedication, and unwavering commitment to the message of Christ. Through his life, Barnabas continues to inspire believers to seek unity, to encourage one another in faith, and to remain steadfast in the teachings of the Gospel. His story, preserved in the Book of Acts and the letters of Paul, remains a powerful reminder of the transformative power of faith and the enduring strength of Christian community.

Chapter 9
Different Perspectives

The figure of Barnabas, layered with history, faith, and mystique, invites a spectrum of interpretations and perspectives. Though little is known about him beyond the New Testament texts, his character and legacy have inspired various views, each emphasizing different aspects of his life and contributions to the early Church. From Christian theologians who honor his foundational role in spreading the Gospel, to Islamic scholars who find in the apocryphal Gospel of Barnabas a bridge between two major world religions, the interpretations of Barnabas's life and legacy reveal as much about the interpreters as they do about Barnabas himself. These perspectives underscore his enduring relevance and the ways in which different faith traditions and scholarly disciplines have engaged with his legacy.

In Christian tradition, Barnabas is widely revered as a saint, an apostle, and a model of humility and encouragement. His story, as recorded in the Book of Acts, presents him as a devoted follower of Christ, a man of deep faith, and a generous spirit who dedicated his life to spreading the Gospel and fostering unity within the early Church. For many Christian theologians and believers, Barnabas represents the qualities of a true disciple—compassion, courage, and a commitment to reconciliation. He is celebrated not only for his missionary journeys alongside Paul but also for his unwavering dedication to inclusivity, as seen in his willingness to embrace Gentile converts and support those who struggled with their faith. This perspective emphasizes Barnabas's role as a mediator, a bridge-builder who sought to heal divisions and unite believers across cultural and religious boundaries.

Within the Catholic and Orthodox traditions, Barnabas holds a special place of veneration. He is often honored as one of the "seventy disciples" mentioned in the Gospel of Luke, and his feast day is celebrated as a testament to his contributions to the early Church. In this context, Barnabas is seen not only as an apostle but also as a saint whose life exemplifies the virtues of charity, humility, and steadfast faith. His decision to sell his land and donate the proceeds to the apostles, as described in Acts, is viewed as a powerful act of renunciation, reflecting his commitment to serving others and dedicating himself fully to the work of God. For many in these traditions, Barnabas is a model of Christian virtue, inspiring believers to embrace a life of generosity, humility, and devotion to the Gospel.

In Protestant circles, Barnabas is similarly respected as a pivotal figure in the early Church, though his legacy is often viewed through the lens of his relationship with Paul and his role in the spread of Christianity. Protestant theologians tend to focus on Barnabas's partnership with Paul, highlighting their joint efforts in evangelism and the impact of their missionary journeys on the growth of the Christian community. Barnabas's decision to advocate for Paul, to support John Mark despite his earlier departure, and to champion the inclusion of Gentiles reflects a spirit of grace and compassion that resonates deeply within the Protestant tradition. Barnabas is seen as a man of conviction, willing to stand up for others even when it meant facing opposition or risking his own reputation.

For many Protestant scholars, Barnabas's legacy is also a reminder of the diversity within the early Church and the ways in which different personalities and perspectives contributed to the development of Christian doctrine and practice. His eventual separation from Paul over their differing views on John Mark is often interpreted as a reflection of the challenges inherent in collaborative ministry, underscoring the idea that unity within the Church does not necessitate uniformity. This perspective sees

Barnabas as a forerunner of the inclusive, ecumenical spirit that has come to define modern Christianity, inspiring believers to embrace diversity while remaining committed to the core teachings of Christ.

In Islamic tradition, Barnabas holds a unique position, largely due to the apocryphal Gospel of Barnabas, which presents a portrayal of Jesus more closely aligned with Islamic views. This text, which diverges significantly from the New Testament Gospels, has led some Muslim scholars and communities to regard Barnabas as an early follower of Jesus who preserved a version of His teachings that is compatible with Islamic theology. The Gospel of Barnabas denies the crucifixion, affirms the oneness of God, and predicts the coming of the prophet Muhammad, all themes that resonate with Islamic beliefs. For some Muslims, this apocryphal gospel represents an alternative account of Jesus's life and teachings, one that validates Islamic perspectives on Jesus as a prophet rather than the Son of God.

It is worth noting that mainstream Islamic scholarship does not universally accept the Gospel of Barnabas as an authoritative text. Most Muslim scholars acknowledge that the gospel is of later origin and do not view it as a reliable historical account of Jesus's life. However, its content has nonetheless sparked interest among Muslims seeking to understand Jesus's role within Islam and the ways in which his teachings might align with their faith. For these readers, the Gospel of Barnabas offers a narrative that bridges some theological gaps between Islam and Christianity, presenting a portrayal of Jesus that emphasizes his prophetic mission and his submission to God's will. This perspective on Barnabas reflects the broader theme of interfaith dialogue and the desire for a shared understanding of Jesus that respects both Christian and Islamic traditions.

The academic community offers yet another perspective on Barnabas, examining him as a historical figure whose life and legacy reveal insights into the social, cultural, and theological dynamics of the early Church. Scholars of early Christianity study Barnabas's role within the apostolic community, analyzing his contributions to the spread of Christianity and his interactions with other apostles. His support for Paul, his role in the Council of Jerusalem, and his efforts to include Gentiles in the faith are viewed as pivotal moments in the development of early Christian doctrine. Through this lens, Barnabas is seen not merely as a disciple but as a key figure who helped shape the inclusive vision of Christianity that would eventually spread across the Roman Empire and beyond.

Academic studies of Barnabas also focus on his legacy as a mediator between Jewish and Gentile Christians, exploring how his background as a Levite from Cyprus positioned him as a bridge between different cultural and religious communities. Scholars note that Barnabas's upbringing in the Hellenistic Jewish community may have influenced his openness to Gentile inclusion, allowing him to navigate the tensions between Jewish traditions and the emerging Christian faith. His commitment to unity, coupled with his willingness to challenge established norms, is seen as a reflection of the adaptive and transformative nature of early Christianity—a movement that sought to transcend cultural and religious boundaries while remaining rooted in the teachings of Jesus.

In addition to his historical significance, scholars have examined the symbolic role of Barnabas in Christian literature and art, where he is often depicted as a figure of encouragement and compassion. His life has inspired numerous artistic representations, from paintings to sculptures, each capturing a different facet of his legacy. In these portrayals, Barnabas is often depicted as a humble yet powerful figure, embodying the values of service, kindness, and dedication to God's mission. These artistic interpretations offer yet another perspective on Barnabas, emphasizing his spiritual virtues and the enduring impact of his life on Christian culture and imagination.

Barnabas's legacy also extends into the realm of ecumenism, where he is often invoked as a model for interfaith dialogue and unity within the Christian community. His role as a mediator, a mentor, and a champion of inclusivity resonates with modern efforts to foster understanding and cooperation among different Christian denominations and religious traditions. For many in the ecumenical movement, Barnabas represents the ideal of a Church that welcomes diversity and values each member's unique contributions. His life serves as an example of how faith can be a force for unity rather than division, a reminder that the essence of the Christian message is one of love, reconciliation, and the pursuit of common ground.

In reflecting on these diverse perspectives, it becomes clear that Barnabas's legacy is as multifaceted as the man himself. His story invites readers and believers from all backgrounds to consider the ways in which faith can transcend boundaries, foster compassion, and embrace the stranger. Whether viewed through the lens of theology, history, art, or interfaith dialogue, Barnabas's life offers valuable lessons on the nature of discipleship, the power of encouragement, and the importance of unity within the Church.

For many, Barnabas remains a symbol of the early Church's expansive vision—a vision that sought to bring together Jews and Gentiles, rich and poor, saints and sinners, under the banner of Christ's love. His legacy, shaped by humility and compassion, continues to inspire believers to live out their faith with courage, grace, and a commitment to unity. Through the various interpretations of his life, Barnabas emerges not only as an apostle of the past but as a figure of enduring relevance, reminding each generation of the transformative power of encouragement and the boundless reach of the Gospel.

As we explore the different perspectives on Barnabas, we are reminded that faith is a journey that encompasses many paths, each offering insights into the divine. His life serves as a testament to the strength found in diversity and the beauty of a faith that welcomes all who seek God's love. Barnabas's story, in all its complexity, invites us to reflect on our own journeys of faith, encouraging us to embrace both unity and diversity, to extend grace to those who struggle, and to remain steadfast in our commitment to the mission of Christ. In this way, Barnabas's legacy lives on, a beacon of hope and inspiration for all who seek to follow in his footsteps.

Chapter 10
Lasting Influence

The influence of Barnabas reaches across centuries, quietly shaping the history and theology of Christianity. Though often overshadowed by more prominent apostles, Barnabas left a legacy that echoes through the practices, values, and spiritual sensibilities of the Christian faith. His role as a mediator, evangelist, and advocate for unity in diversity created a path that would influence early Christian communities and guide the Church in navigating the complex landscape of religious and cultural differences. Today, Barnabas's legacy remains alive in the principles he embodied: compassion, inclusion, resilience, and a tireless commitment to the Gospel.

Barnabas's enduring influence begins with his fundamental approach to discipleship. The Book of Acts introduces him as "a good man, full of the Holy Spirit and faith," a title that speaks to his character and spiritual depth. He was not only a fervent believer but also a true disciple who lived out the teachings of Christ in both word and deed. His decision to sell his property and give the proceeds to the apostles reveals his profound commitment to Christian communal life, where material possessions were shared, and individual needs were met with collective resources. Barnabas's life of generosity inspired early Christians to live simply and to prioritize spiritual wealth over material gain, a theme that would resonate through the early Church and continue to inspire movements of self-sacrifice and communal care throughout Christian history.

In addition to his generosity, Barnabas's example as a mentor to emerging leaders has had a lasting impact on Christian leadership models. His relationship with Paul, and later with John Mark, highlights his role as a nurturing, supportive figure—a leader who encouraged others and helped them realize their potential. When Paul, once a notorious persecutor of Christians, sought acceptance among the apostles, it was Barnabas who first stood by him, vouching for the authenticity of his conversion. By doing so, Barnabas enabled Paul's entrance into the Christian community, paving the way for his extraordinary ministry. This act of encouragement was not a simple gesture; it was a transformative moment that shaped the future of the Church and established Barnabas as a model of inclusive leadership, demonstrating that faith was not bound by one's past but could bring renewal and redemption to all.

Barnabas's approach to mentorship extended beyond Paul to include his relative, John Mark, a young man whose journey of faith faced challenges and setbacks. When John Mark left their first missionary journey and wished to rejoin later, Paul's disappointment led him to refuse. Barnabas, however, saw potential in John Mark and chose to take him under his wing, giving him a second chance. This decision cost Barnabas his partnership with Paul, yet it also highlighted his commitment to nurturing emerging disciples, regardless of their failures. In this way, Barnabas championed a form of leadership rooted in patience, grace, and a belief in the redemptive power of God's love—a legacy that resonates with Christian educators, pastors, and mentors who seek to guide others with compassion.

The influence of Barnabas also extends to the theological direction of the early Church, particularly in the inclusion of Gentiles. As one of the first to advocate for Gentile believers, Barnabas played a vital role in broadening the scope of Christianity beyond the Jewish community. His work in Antioch, a city with a diverse population, revealed his belief that the Gospel was meant for all, regardless of cultural or ethnic background. Barnabas's conviction that Gentiles should not be bound by Jewish ceremonial laws was instrumental in shaping early Christian identity, affirming that salvation was based on faith in Christ rather than adherence to traditional rites. This inclusive stance foreshadowed the global reach of Christianity, setting a precedent for a Church that transcends boundaries and unites believers across differences.

The Council of Jerusalem, one of the first formal gatherings to address doctrinal issues, bears the mark of Barnabas's influence. He stood with Paul to argue that Gentile converts should not be required to follow all Jewish customs, including circumcision. This decision, affirmed by the council, reinforced the Church's commitment to unity and inclusivity, recognizing that the message of Jesus was not bound by cultural practices but was accessible to all who believed. The Council's decision to welcome Gentiles without imposing additional burdens allowed Christianity to grow beyond its initial cultural confines, establishing it as a faith that valued spiritual kinship over ethnic ties. Barnabas's stance at the Council laid the groundwork for future discussions on inclusion, unity, and doctrinal adaptability, themes that would guide the Church as it expanded across regions and adapted to diverse cultures.

Barnabas's missionary efforts also influenced the spread of Christianity to new territories, helping establish vibrant communities in regions previously untouched by the Gospel. His travels with Paul brought the message of Christ to cities like Antioch, Iconium, Lystra, and Derbe, where they established communities that would serve as centers of Christian life. Through preaching, teaching, and organizing these early churches, Barnabas helped create a network of believers that would endure even after his departure, a testament to the strength of his dedication and the impact of his ministry. These communities, inspired by his inclusive vision and compassionate leadership, became beacons of faith, fostering unity among believers and serving as models for other Christian congregations to follow.

The legacy of Barnabas's missions is also reflected in the resilience and endurance of early Christian communities, which faced frequent persecution. Barnabas exemplified courage and perseverance, qualities that would become essential to the survival of the Church. In a time when believers were often marginalized, threatened, and at risk of persecution, Barnabas's steadfast faith and willingness to confront adversity inspired others to hold fast to their beliefs. His example encouraged early Christians to endure hardship with grace, knowing that their faith was stronger than any opposition they might face. This spirit of resilience, rooted in Barnabas's own experiences, became a cornerstone of Christian identity, fostering a Church that could withstand trials and emerge even stronger.

Barnabas's influence also extends to the principles of Christian peacemaking and reconciliation. Known as a "son of encouragement," Barnabas consistently worked to resolve conflicts and build bridges within the early Church. His role as a mediator between Jewish and Gentile believers, as well as between the apostles and new converts, reflected his deep commitment to unity. Barnabas understood that the Church, as the body of Christ, was strongest when it embraced diversity and fostered mutual respect. His example as a peacemaker set a precedent for future leaders, demonstrating that disagreements and differences could be resolved through dialogue, empathy, and a shared commitment to the Gospel. This legacy of reconciliation remains a guiding principle within Christian communities, inspiring efforts toward unity, healing, and ecumenism.

Barnabas's emphasis on grace and second chances has influenced the Church's approach to repentance, forgiveness, and personal growth. His willingness to mentor John Mark, despite his earlier failure, reflects a deep belief in the potential for change and the power of forgiveness. Barnabas's actions remind believers that Christianity is a faith of redemption, where past mistakes do not define one's future. His legacy encourages Christians to approach others with grace, to see beyond faults, and to offer support as they seek to grow in their faith. This compassionate view has had a lasting impact on Christian pastoral care, emphasizing that the Church should be a place of healing and renewal, where individuals are encouraged to find purpose, redemption, and restoration in the love of God.

In the broader context of Christian history, Barnabas's influence is also seen in his dedication to simplicity, charity, and communal life. His early decision to sell his land and contribute to the needs of the community has inspired countless acts of generosity and self-sacrifice throughout Christian history. Monastic movements, charitable organizations, and communal Christian living all echo Barnabas's example of selflessness, reminding believers that true discipleship often involves placing the needs of others above one's own. His legacy calls Christians to a life of service, one that prioritizes spiritual wealth over material gain and values relationships over possessions.

Barnabas's legacy further extends to the ecumenical and interfaith movements, where his spirit of inclusion and unity continues to resonate. As a figure who sought to bridge divides, Barnabas's example inspires efforts to foster dialogue and understanding among different Christian denominations and even between Christianity and other religions. His commitment to bringing diverse believers together reflects an approach to faith that values unity without erasing difference, a vision that has inspired modern ecumenical efforts to bring Christians of various traditions into closer fellowship. His example also encourages interfaith dialogue, fostering respect and mutual understanding between Christianity and other faiths in the spirit of peace and cooperation.

Through all these facets of his life and legacy, Barnabas remains a figure of profound influence, a quiet yet powerful presence whose actions have shaped the course of Christian history in countless ways. His commitment to encouragement, inclusivity, and compassion continues to inspire believers to live out the Gospel with humility and grace, to embrace diversity, and to work for unity within the Church. For Barnabas, the message of Christ was not simply a set of doctrines; it was a way of life, a call to love, serve, and uplift others. His legacy is a reminder that true faith is not measured by one's position or prominence but by the depth of one's commitment to God and to the well-being of others.

As we reflect on Barnabas's influence, we see in him a model of discipleship that is both challenging and inspiring. His life encourages believers to embrace a faith that is expansive, resilient, and deeply rooted in love. In a world often marked by division, his legacy invites Christians to pursue reconciliation, to extend grace, and to stand alongside those who seek redemption and healing. Through his actions, Barnabas leaves a lasting imprint on the Church, a testament to the enduring power of faith, humility, and the boundless reach of God's love.

In the end, Barnabas's lasting influence is not confined to his historical contributions but lives on in the hearts and lives of those who seek to follow his example. His legacy calls believers to a higher standard of compassion, a deeper commitment to unity, and a life dedicated to the service of others. Barnabas, though often standing in the shadows of history, remains a pillar of the early Church—a quiet yet powerful testament to the transformative power of a life lived in faith. Through his story, Christians are reminded that the truest expressions of faith are found in acts of love, kindness, and encouragement, qualities that continue to illuminate the path of discipleship today.

Chapter 11
Martyr of Faith

The final years of Barnabas's life are shrouded in both mystery and reverence. As one of the earliest apostles and a cornerstone of the Christian community, Barnabas remained committed to his faith, his mission, and the teachings of Christ until the very end. His story, rich with acts of courage, compassion, and dedication, culminates in a death that is believed to have inspired and emboldened believers for generations. Though historical records provide only sparse details, early Christian tradition holds that Barnabas met a martyr's death, a fate that elevated him as an exemplar of faith and devotion. His martyrdom, veiled in legend, endures as a symbol of ultimate sacrifice for the Gospel and a testament to his unwavering commitment to the path he chose to follow.

In tracing the tradition of Barnabas's martyrdom, many scholars turn to early Christian accounts that describe his final mission in his homeland, Cyprus. According to these accounts, Barnabas returned to Cyprus, not only to spread the message of Christ but to tend to the community he had helped establish. Cyprus held deep significance for Barnabas, as it was where his journey began, the place of his roots, and a land where his influence was both respected and tested. His return to Cyprus signifies a full-circle moment—a testament to his enduring love for his people and his commitment to ensuring that the Gospel took root in every corner of his homeland.

The account of Barnabas's death reveals the perils that early Christians faced, particularly in regions where tensions between traditional beliefs and the emerging Christian faith were high. According to tradition, Barnabas's success in spreading the Gospel in Cyprus angered certain local authorities and religious leaders who viewed his teachings as a threat to established customs. His presence stirred opposition, likely fueled by the fear that his message of a risen Christ and a new covenant was undermining traditional beliefs. The extent of this opposition would soon become tragically evident as Barnabas found himself facing those who saw his faith not as a source of truth but as a dangerous deviation from their own traditions.

While details vary, one prevailing account of Barnabas's death describes his capture by a group of hostile individuals who opposed his teachings. Despite their efforts to silence him, Barnabas reportedly remained steadfast, refusing to recant or compromise his faith. His captors ultimately took his life, marking his end as that of a martyr. Some accounts claim that he was stoned to death, a brutal yet symbolic method of execution often reserved for those seen as agitators or heretics. In standing firm until his final breath, Barnabas demonstrated the depth of his faith, offering the ultimate testament to his devotion to Christ.

Another tradition asserts that Barnabas's body was hidden and later discovered by followers who carefully preserved his remains. Early sources suggest that his followers buried him with a copy of the Gospel of Matthew, symbolizing his dedication to the teachings of Christ and his desire for these teachings to continue beyond his death. This burial, shrouded in reverence and mystery, reflects the early Christian practice of honoring martyrs as individuals whose lives and deaths bore witness to the power of faith. The relic of Barnabas, accompanied by a gospel, would come to hold deep symbolic value, representing the link between the written Word and the living faith that he embodied.

The martyrdom of Barnabas holds a profound place in Christian tradition, not only for the sacrifice it represents but for the devotion it inspired among early believers. The martyrdom of an apostle like Barnabas reinforced the idea that faith was not simply a matter of belief but a commitment that transcended life itself. His death served as a rallying point, encouraging others to remain steadfast in their convictions, regardless of the cost. In a time when Christians were often marginalized, persecuted, and misunderstood, the death of Barnabas sent a powerful message that the Gospel was worth any sacrifice. For the early Church, Barnabas's martyrdom was not a defeat but a victory of faith over fear, of truth over opposition.

The story of Barnabas's martyrdom also resonates with the broader theme of Christian endurance in the face of persecution. His death stands alongside those of other early martyrs who chose faith over life, knowing that their actions would strengthen the resolve of their fellow believers. In Barnabas, the early Church found a figure who exemplified resilience, courage, and an unbreakable bond with Christ. His willingness to lay down his life for his faith transformed him from a respected teacher and apostle into a symbol of unyielding devotion, inspiring generations of believers to embrace their faith with similar courage.

Barnabas's martyrdom had a lasting impact on the early Christian community in Cyprus, which honored his memory and looked to him as a protector and intercessor. Over time, the memory of his life and death became intertwined with the collective identity of Cypriot Christians, who regarded him as their patron saint and a guiding spirit. Barnabas's influence on the island persisted for centuries, shaping the character and resilience of the Christian community there. His story of sacrifice reminded believers that the cost of faith was great, yet the rewards were greater still. This reverence for Barnabas as a martyr contributed to the resilience of the Christian faith in Cyprus and beyond, offering a source of strength and hope for those who faced persecution in later centuries.

Beyond Cyprus, the legacy of Barnabas's martyrdom extended throughout the early Church, where accounts of his death inspired believers facing similar challenges. In Barnabas, Christians saw a reflection of their own struggles, a reminder that their faith was part of a larger story of sacrifice and redemption.

His death symbolized the profound cost of discipleship, an unbreakable bond with Christ that no earthly power could sever. As tales of his martyrdom spread, they became part of the collective memory of the Church, a reminder that the message of Christ endured not only through words but through the lives and sacrifices of those who carried it forward.

The devotion inspired by Barnabas's martyrdom also shaped the practices of honoring saints and martyrs within the Church. The preservation of his memory and the reverence shown to his remains reflect the early Christian tradition of venerating those who had given their lives for the faith. Barnabas's story became part of the tapestry of martyrdom narratives that reminded believers of the strength found in unity, the hope found in resurrection, and the love found in Christ's sacrifice. His martyrdom thus became both a historical event and a spiritual symbol, a reminder of the transformative power of faith and the enduring strength of the Christian community.

Barnabas's death as a martyr was not the end of his influence but the beginning of a legacy that would inspire countless others to pursue their faith with courage. His life, marked by compassion and dedication, was crowned by a death that underscored the ultimate sacrifice he was willing to make. In dying for his faith, Barnabas joined the ranks of those who, in the words of the Book of Revelation, "did not love their lives so much as to shrink from death." His martyrdom stands as a reminder that true faith is a journey that demands everything, yet offers the promise of eternal life in return.

For Barnabas, martyrdom was not simply the price of his convictions but the final affirmation of his life's work. Through his death, he bore witness to the message of Christ in the most profound way possible, sealing his testimony with his own blood. His martyrdom invites reflection on the meaning of discipleship, the cost of following Christ, and the hope that sustains believers even in the face of death. In Barnabas, the early Church saw a model of faith that was unwavering, a spirit that was unbreakable, and a love for Christ that transcended all earthly fears.

The martyrdom of Barnabas continues to inspire Christians who seek to understand the depths of commitment, sacrifice, and faith. His story challenges believers to consider what they are willing to give for their faith and reminds them that the path of discipleship is not always easy, but it is always worthwhile. Through his life and death, Barnabas left a legacy that speaks to the power of faith, the strength of community, and the eternal hope found in Christ. His martyrdom stands as a testament to the transformative power of the Gospel and the unbreakable bond between the believer and the Savior.

Chapter 12
Friend of God

Among the early figures of the Christian faith, Barnabas stands out not only as an apostle and martyr but as one who is remembered for his profound spiritual intimacy with God. The bond Barnabas shared with the Divine was not a distant relationship based solely on doctrine; it was an intimate, lived connection that suffused his entire life with purpose, strength, and compassion. To understand Barnabas as a friend of God is to look beyond his actions as a missionary and evangelist and to recognize the deep spiritual life that animated his journey, one characterized by trust, humility, and a profound sense of calling. His friendship with God is woven throughout his story, revealing a spirituality that serves as both a model and an inspiration for those who seek a closer relationship with the Divine.

The foundation of Barnabas's friendship with God can be traced to his early life and spiritual formation, nurtured within the Jewish faith and its traditions. As a Levite from Cyprus, Barnabas was steeped in the practices of prayer, study, and reverence for the sacred texts. This upbringing instilled in him a deep sense of devotion to God, which only grew more profound with his acceptance of Jesus as the promised Messiah. Through Christ, Barnabas experienced a renewal of faith that did not abandon his Jewish roots but rather fulfilled and expanded them. In Christ, Barnabas found a path that deepened his connection with God, leading him toward a relationship marked by personal devotion and a readiness to act upon divine inspiration.

The nature of Barnabas's friendship with God was evident in his actions and choices throughout his life. Barnabas did not merely preach the message of Christ; he embodied it, living a life of sacrifice, humility, and unwavering faith. His decision to sell his land and offer the proceeds to the early Christian community was a tangible expression of his trust in God's provision, a statement that his reliance was on the Divine rather than on material wealth. This act of generosity was more than charity; it was a gesture of surrender, a way of placing his life in God's hands and allowing himself to be guided entirely by his spiritual calling. Through such acts, Barnabas demonstrated that his friendship with God was one of complete trust, a relationship that left no room for half-measures or reservations.

Barnabas's openness to the Holy Spirit further illustrates the depth of his connection with God. Throughout the Book of Acts, we see him portrayed as a man full of faith and the Holy Spirit, someone who was attuned to divine guidance in all his endeavors. His friendship with God was not limited to prayer or private devotion; it extended into his ministry, guiding his actions and decisions. When the Christian community in Jerusalem sent him to Antioch, Barnabas responded without hesitation, trusting that this call was divinely inspired. In Antioch, he witnessed the grace of God among the Gentiles and immediately recognized it as the work of the Spirit, encouraging and nurturing the faith of these new believers. His ability to perceive and respond to God's presence in unexpected places underscores the closeness of his relationship with the Divine, a friendship that enabled him to see beyond cultural and religious boundaries to the heart of God's purpose.

This closeness to God also shaped Barnabas's interactions with others, particularly his role as a mentor and encourager. His relationship with Paul, marked by compassion and support, reflects Barnabas's ability to see the potential in others and to nurture their gifts. His willingness to advocate for Paul when others were wary demonstrates a divine perspective, one that sees beyond surface judgments to the potential within each person.

Similarly, his patience with John Mark reveals a deep understanding of God's redemptive grace, a belief that every individual has the capacity for growth and renewal. Barnabas's mentorship was an extension of his friendship with God—a way of embodying the Divine's compassion, forgiveness, and encouragement. In Barnabas, those he guided saw a reflection of God's patience and unwavering support, qualities that transformed their own lives and strengthened their faith.

Barnabas's spirituality was not one of self-centered mysticism but of active service, a life lived in constant communion with God and directed toward others. His friendship with God was evident in his role as a reconciler, someone who bridged divides within the Church and fostered unity among believers. He understood that true faith calls for harmony and mutual respect, a conviction that guided his efforts to include Gentiles in the Christian community and to mediate conflicts within the Church. This commitment to unity was not merely a matter of organizational stability; it was a reflection of the unity he experienced in his relationship with God. Barnabas's friendship with God overflowed into his love for others, embodying Christ's command to love one's neighbor as oneself. His peacemaking efforts, his encouragement of new believers, and his willingness to endure hardship for the sake of the Gospel all reveal a soul profoundly attuned to God's will and dedicated to living out that divine friendship in tangible ways.

The depth of Barnabas's spirituality is perhaps best reflected in his unwavering faith during times of adversity. Barnabas's friendship with God provided him with a source of strength that carried him through moments of rejection, persecution, and even martyrdom. His resilience in the face of hardship was not born of human determination alone; it was the fruit of a relationship rooted in trust and love. Barnabas understood that his life was held in God's hands, and this assurance freed him from fear, allowing him to pursue his mission with courage and steadfastness. Even when his partnership with Paul ended in disagreement, Barnabas continued his work with the same dedication, trusting that God's purposes would prevail despite human differences. His ability to navigate these challenges with grace reveals a soul that was anchored in divine friendship, a faith that could not be shaken by external circumstances.

For Barnabas, being a friend of God meant embracing a life of selflessness and surrender, qualities that drew others to him and inspired them to seek a similar closeness with the Divine. His life was a testament to the idea that friendship with God is not a solitary pursuit but one that overflows into every relationship, every act of service, and every moment of faith. Barnabas's journey demonstrates that true intimacy with God transforms not only the individual but also the community, creating ripples of grace that extend far beyond the individual soul. In his friendship with God, Barnabas found the courage to embrace a path of radical love, a journey that ultimately led him to lay down his life for his faith.

Barnabas's story invites believers to reflect on the nature of their own relationship with God, challenging them to pursue a friendship that is as deep, transformative, and life-giving as his. His example reminds us that a true friend of God is someone who embodies the values of compassion, humility, and courage, someone who lives out their faith not only through words but through actions that reflect the Divine's love. In Barnabas, we see a model of spiritual friendship that is accessible to all—a reminder that God's friendship is open to anyone willing to seek it, nurture it, and live it out in the world.

In the centuries since Barnabas's life, his friendship with God has continued to inspire believers, reminding them of the joy, peace, and strength that come from a life rooted in divine love. His example encourages Christians to pursue a spirituality that is both intimate and active, one that finds expression in service, community, and unwavering trust. Barnabas's friendship with God is a legacy that endures, a call to every believer to walk closely with the Divine, to be guided by God's presence, and to live a life that reflects the light of Christ.

Through his life and example, Barnabas reveals that friendship with God is not reserved for a select few but is available to all who seek it sincerely. His story is a testament to the power of faith, the beauty of surrender, and the transformative impact of a soul attuned to God's will. In Barnabas, we find a friend of God whose life continues to speak to the Church, inviting believers to pursue a relationship with the Divine that is as genuine, courageous, and loving as his own.

Chapter 13
Defender of Unity in the Early Church

The early Church, vibrant and expanding, was also fraught with internal tensions. As the Christian message spread, believers from diverse backgrounds—Jewish and Gentile, rich and poor, educated and uneducated—came together to form a new kind of community. These early followers of Christ held to a revolutionary faith, but they also faced challenges as they sought to reconcile different cultural traditions, beliefs, and practices. In this setting, Barnabas emerged as one of the most steadfast defenders of unity. His approach to leadership was marked by an emphasis on harmony, inclusion, and reconciliation, qualities that would prove essential in helping the fledgling Church survive and thrive amidst its growing pains.

Barnabas's commitment to unity was rooted in his own background and character. As a Levite from Cyprus, he was familiar with the Jewish traditions that defined the earliest Christian believers, yet he was also raised in a Hellenistic, multicultural environment. This unique upbringing equipped Barnabas with a broad perspective and an openness that allowed him to move comfortably between different worlds. His early exposure to diverse customs and ways of thinking enabled him to understand the importance of unity within diversity, an understanding that would guide his work in the Church. Barnabas knew that the Christian message was one of universality, a message that transcended ethnic and cultural boundaries. His commitment to unity was not merely organizational; it was a reflection of the Gospel itself, which called for love and mutual acceptance among all believers.

The first major test of Barnabas's commitment to unity came in Antioch, where a new Christian community had begun to flourish. This community included a significant number of Gentile converts—people who had embraced the teachings of Jesus but did not adhere to Jewish customs. When Barnabas arrived in Antioch, sent by the apostles to observe and support this growing congregation, he encountered a diverse group of believers whose practices were unlike those of the Jewish Christians in Jerusalem. Rather than responding with suspicion or criticism, Barnabas welcomed this diversity, recognizing the grace of God at work among the Gentiles. His acceptance of these new believers demonstrated a willingness to see beyond cultural differences and embrace a faith that united rather than divided.

In Antioch, Barnabas's role as a defender of unity became clear. He encouraged the Gentile believers to remain true to the teachings of Jesus, affirming that their faith did not require them to adopt Jewish customs. This stance would become increasingly significant as more Gentiles joined the Christian movement, raising questions about the relationship between Jewish traditions and the new faith. Barnabas's openness to these Gentile believers laid the groundwork for an inclusive Church, one that could embrace people from all backgrounds without forcing them into a single cultural mold. His approach reflected the essence of the Gospel, which called for a community built not on uniformity but on shared faith, love, and commitment to Christ.

Barnabas's efforts to maintain unity among believers would reach a critical point at the Council of Jerusalem. This gathering, one of the first major councils in Christian history, was convened to address the question of whether Gentile converts should be required to follow Jewish laws, such as circumcision. The issue threatened to divide the early Church, as some Jewish Christians believed that adherence to these customs was essential, while others argued that faith in Christ alone was sufficient. The debate was intense, and the stakes were high: the future of the

Church's inclusivity and its ability to reach people beyond the Jewish community depended on the outcome.

At the Council, Barnabas stood alongside Paul to advocate for the Gentiles, arguing that they should not be burdened with requirements that were culturally specific to Judaism. Their argument was not one of opposition to Jewish tradition, but rather an affirmation of the Gospel's universality. Barnabas understood that the message of Christ transcended cultural boundaries, and he believed that the unity of the Church depended on its ability to welcome believers from all backgrounds without imposing additional burdens. His stance at the Council of Jerusalem reflected his deep commitment to inclusivity and his conviction that the Gospel was meant for all people, regardless of their cultural or religious heritage.

The decision of the Council to accept Gentiles without requiring circumcision was a turning point in Christian history, one that affirmed the Church's commitment to unity within diversity. Barnabas's role in this decision underscores his influence as a defender of unity, someone who saw the bigger picture and was willing to challenge established norms to ensure that the Church remained inclusive. His advocacy for the Gentiles was not simply a matter of pragmatism; it was a reflection of his belief in a Church that could accommodate different expressions of faith while remaining rooted in the teachings of Christ. Through his actions at the Council, Barnabas helped set a precedent for future generations, demonstrating that unity could be maintained without erasing cultural differences.

Barnabas's commitment to unity extended beyond doctrinal debates to his personal relationships within the Church. His ability to work alongside people with different perspectives, such as Paul, illustrates his willingness to embrace diversity within the body of believers. Barnabas and Paul shared a common mission, yet their personalities and approaches to ministry were distinct. Barnabas, known for his patience and empathy, balanced Paul's intense and sometimes uncompromising zeal. Their partnership was a model of complementary strengths, showing that unity did not require uniformity but could thrive through collaboration and mutual respect.

Even when Barnabas and Paul eventually parted ways over a disagreement regarding John Mark, Barnabas remained committed to unity. Their separation, while painful, was not born out of animosity but out of differing visions for ministry. Barnabas's decision to take John Mark and continue his mission reflects his belief in the importance of nurturing each member of the Christian community, even those who had stumbled. His actions demonstrated that unity could coexist with personal differences, that the mission of the Church was broad enough to encompass various paths. Barnabas's commitment to John Mark, and his willingness to continue his work despite the separation from Paul, illustrate his unwavering dedication to fostering a diverse yet united community of believers.

Barnabas's role as a defender of unity within the early Church was grounded in his understanding of the Gospel as a message of reconciliation. He believed that faith in Christ brought people together, breaking down the barriers of ethnicity, culture, and tradition. His work among Jewish and Gentile believers alike reflects this conviction, showing that unity was not merely a goal but an intrinsic part of the Christian faith. For Barnabas, the Church was not simply a collection of individuals but a single body united by love and purpose. His commitment to unity was a reflection of his belief that the Church was a living expression of Christ's presence in the world—a presence that could not be divided by human distinctions.

Barnabas's legacy as a defender of unity has continued to inspire the Church throughout its history. His example reminds believers that the true strength of the Church lies in its ability to embrace diversity, to welcome people from all walks of life, and to unite them in a common faith. In a world often divided by cultural, social, and ideological differences, Barnabas's vision of unity offers a powerful reminder of the Gospel's capacity to transcend divisions and bring people together. His life and ministry challenge Christians to seek reconciliation, to build bridges, and to work for harmony within the body of Christ.

In modern times, Barnabas's legacy as a defender of unity remains profoundly relevant. His approach to leadership, marked by compassion, openness, and a willingness to embrace diversity, provides a model for addressing the challenges faced by the Church today. As believers continue to navigate questions of identity, inclusivity, and tradition, Barnabas's example calls them to prioritize unity, to see each other as members of a single family bound by faith in Christ. His life encourages Christians to look beyond differences, to seek common ground, and to celebrate the diversity that enriches the Church.

Barnabas's role in the early Church as a unifying figure reflects his deep understanding of the Gospel as a call to love, acceptance, and reconciliation. His commitment to unity was not an abstract ideal but a lived reality, one that shaped his interactions, his decisions, and his ministry. Through his example, Barnabas invites believers to embrace a faith that brings people together, a faith that celebrates diversity while holding fast to the truth of Christ. His legacy as a defender of unity endures as a beacon of hope and a reminder that the Church, despite its differences, is strongest when it stands together as one.

Chapter 14
Mentor of Leaders

In the story of Barnabas, we find a leader whose influence extended not only through his missionary journeys and doctrinal positions but through the personal relationships he cultivated with others. Among the most significant aspects of Barnabas's legacy is his role as a mentor, particularly to prominent figures such as Paul and John Mark, whose ministries would shape the early Christian Church. Barnabas's nurturing approach, characterized by encouragement, patience, and a keen ability to see potential in others, reflects a deep understanding of the role mentorship plays in the growth of faith communities. His guidance helped shape the leaders of the early Church, offering a model of mentorship that continues to inspire Christian leaders today.

The mentorship between Barnabas and Paul stands as one of the most influential relationships in the New Testament. Before he became the Apostle Paul, Saul of Tarsus was known as a fierce persecutor of Christians. After his dramatic conversion on the road to Damascus, Paul was met with fear and suspicion from the Christian community. His past actions had left an indelible mark, and many doubted the sincerity of his transformation. It was Barnabas who bridged this gap of mistrust, extending a hand of friendship and guiding Paul through the difficult process of integrating into the Christian community. By vouching for Paul and introducing him to the apostles, Barnabas provided him with the opportunity to begin his ministry, a gesture that would prove transformative not only for Paul but for the future of Christianity.

Barnabas's decision to mentor Paul was not merely an act of kindness; it was a profound recognition of the potential that lay within Paul's newly redirected zeal. Barnabas saw beyond Paul's past and understood the magnitude of his conversion. His willingness to advocate for Paul, even at the risk of his own reputation, highlights his dedication to nurturing leaders who could advance the Gospel. By extending grace to Paul and offering him a fresh start, Barnabas exemplified the power of mentorship rooted in forgiveness and vision. He understood that a true mentor is not merely a teacher but a guide who walks alongside others, helping them to find their voice and purpose within the community of faith.

Through their missionary journeys, Barnabas continued to support and guide Paul, helping him navigate the challenges and complexities of ministry. Their collaboration was marked by mutual respect, as Barnabas encouraged Paul to step into his role as a teacher and leader. Rather than competing for prominence, Barnabas selflessly allowed Paul to take the lead, especially as Paul's gifts and calling became more evident. This humility underscores Barnabas's unique approach to mentorship—one that prioritizes the success and growth of others over personal recognition. His relationship with Paul demonstrates that mentorship within the Christian community is not about control but about fostering independence and helping others fulfill their divine calling.

Barnabas's mentorship extended beyond Paul to include another prominent figure in the early Church: John Mark. This young man, who was also Barnabas's relative, began his journey with high hopes and enthusiasm but soon encountered difficulties. On one of their early missions, John Mark abandoned the journey, an action that deeply disappointed Paul. When John Mark later sought to rejoin them, Paul resisted, viewing his previous departure as a sign of unreliability. Barnabas, however, saw something different in John Mark—a potential that was worth nurturing despite his early setback. Rather than dismissing him,

Barnabas chose to take him under his wing, offering him a second chance to grow and learn from his mistakes.

This decision to mentor John Mark, even in the face of Paul's strong objections, reveals the depth of Barnabas's commitment to mentorship as an act of grace and patience. Barnabas understood that leadership is a process that often involves setbacks and growth. He believed in the potential for transformation, not just for Paul but for John Mark as well. His willingness to invest in John Mark's development, despite his initial failure, exemplifies a mentorship grounded in compassion and long-term vision. For Barnabas, mentorship was not conditional upon perfection; rather, it was an opportunity to walk alongside others, encouraging them through challenges and guiding them toward maturity.

In time, Barnabas's mentorship of John Mark bore fruit in unexpected ways. John Mark would go on to become a respected figure in the Christian community, and many scholars believe he is the author of the Gospel of Mark, one of the four canonical Gospels. This remarkable transformation illustrates the power of Barnabas's patient, faith-driven approach to mentorship. By believing in John Mark's potential and offering him the support he needed, Barnabas helped cultivate a leader whose contributions would resonate throughout Christian history. His mentorship reminds us that the impact of nurturing others often extends far beyond our immediate efforts, shaping lives and legacies that can inspire future generations.

The mentorship style of Barnabas reflects a profound understanding of what it means to nurture leadership within a faith community. Unlike traditional models of authority that focus on hierarchy and control, Barnabas's approach was rooted in encouragement and empowerment. He did not seek to impose his own views or methods but rather aimed to draw out the unique gifts and callings of those he mentored. This approach, characterized by humility and a genuine desire to see others succeed, stands in contrast to leadership styles that prioritize personal power. For Barnabas, mentorship was about cultivating the potential within others, helping them find their own path and their own voice within the mission of the Church.

Barnabas's legacy as a mentor also underscores the importance of resilience in Christian leadership. His commitment to guiding others, even when they faltered, demonstrates that true mentorship requires patience, empathy, and a willingness to walk through challenges alongside those in one's care. Barnabas's mentorship was not about perfection or immediate success; it was about fostering growth, supporting others through their struggles, and remaining steadfast in the belief that God's grace is sufficient to transform even the most imperfect individuals. His approach encourages Christian leaders to embrace the journey of faith as a process, one that allows for mistakes, learning, and continual growth.

In addition to shaping the lives of individual leaders, Barnabas's mentorship had a profound impact on the broader Church community. By nurturing Paul, he helped establish one of the most influential voices in Christian theology, one whose teachings would shape the understanding of grace, salvation, and the nature of the Church for centuries to come. By mentoring John Mark, Barnabas played a role in the creation of a Gospel that continues to inspire and guide believers around the world. His influence reached beyond the immediate impact of his own ministry, contributing to the foundation of a faith community that would continue to grow and flourish. Through his mentorship, Barnabas helped lay the groundwork for a Church that valued diversity, encouraged growth, and embraced believers from all walks of life.

The story of Barnabas as a mentor serves as a powerful reminder of the importance of investing in others within the Christian community. His life invites believers to consider how they, too, can support and encourage those around them, nurturing the next generation of leaders who will carry forward the message of Christ. Barnabas's example calls Christians to view mentorship not as a duty but as a privilege—an opportunity to participate in God's work by helping others discover and fulfill their calling.

His legacy challenges believers to approach mentorship with humility, compassion, and a willingness to see the potential in each person, regardless of their past or present struggles.

In the centuries since Barnabas's life, his approach to mentorship has continued to inspire Christian leaders, educators, and mentors who seek to guide others in their journey of faith. His example encourages believers to embrace a mentorship model that is rooted in love, guided by patience, and committed to the growth and success of those they serve. By following the path laid out by Barnabas, Christians are reminded that leadership within the Church is not about personal achievement but about lifting others up, helping them to realize their potential and to contribute to the life of the community.

Barnabas's role as a mentor reflects his deep understanding of the nature of Christian discipleship. He recognized that faith is a journey that requires support, guidance, and the encouragement of others. His life offers a vision of a Church that is not built on the talents of a few but on the collective strength of a community united in purpose. Barnabas's legacy as a mentor invites believers to embrace this vision, to see themselves not only as individuals in faith but as part of a larger body, each member supporting and uplifting the other.

As a mentor of leaders, Barnabas leaves a legacy that transcends time, inspiring Christians to invest in the lives of others with faith and patience. His life teaches that the greatest impact often comes not from solitary achievements but from the relationships we cultivate and the lives we touch. Through his mentorship, Barnabas became a bridge between generations of believers, linking his own time with the future of the Church. His example encourages Christians to look beyond their own accomplishments and to see the lasting value in guiding, nurturing, and supporting those who will continue the work of faith.

Chapter 15
Diplomat of Faith

In the emerging Christian community, where diverse beliefs and backgrounds often led to tension, Barnabas became a diplomat of faith—a man who skillfully navigated disagreements and bridged divides within the early Church. His reputation for wisdom, patience, and empathy enabled him to handle delicate situations with a calmness that garnered respect from believers across cultural and doctrinal divides. His actions and approach reveal a man deeply committed to peace, a leader who understood that unity was essential for the Church's survival and growth. In Barnabas, we see a model of diplomacy that was as much spiritual as it was practical, reflecting a profound dedication to preserving harmony while remaining steadfast in the teachings of Christ.

Barnabas's role as a diplomat was first evident during his early work in Antioch, where he encountered a vibrant yet culturally mixed congregation of Jews and Gentiles. These two groups brought their own customs, traditions, and interpretations of faith, creating a rich but potentially divisive environment. When Barnabas arrived in Antioch, he recognized the grace of God in this diverse community and encouraged both Jewish and Gentile believers to embrace one another as brothers and sisters in Christ. He understood that the strength of the Church lay in its inclusivity, in its ability to welcome people from all walks of life into a single, united body of faith.

As a diplomat, Barnabas was not content with merely acknowledging diversity; he actively worked to bridge the divides it could cause. His approach to the Gentile believers in Antioch reflects his belief in the importance of unity without forced conformity. Rather than insisting that the Gentile converts adopt all Jewish customs, Barnabas encouraged them to focus on faith in Christ as the foundation of their identity as Christians. This perspective was a radical departure from the traditional Jewish requirements, emphasizing a faith centered on the heart and spirit rather than external rituals. Barnabas's diplomacy in Antioch set a precedent for a Church that could thrive in diversity, united by a common faith that transcended cultural practices.

One of Barnabas's greatest acts of diplomacy took place at the Council of Jerusalem, where a critical debate arose over whether Gentile converts needed to adhere to Jewish law, including practices like circumcision. The controversy threatened to divide the Church, as Jewish Christians from Jerusalem insisted on the need for traditional observance, while others, like Paul and Barnabas, argued that salvation was through faith alone and should not be burdened with additional requirements. This debate represented more than a theological disagreement; it was a question of identity, of whether Christianity would remain a subset of Judaism or expand into a faith accessible to all.

At the Council, Barnabas played a vital role in advocating for the Gentile believers, presenting their experiences and affirming that the Holy Spirit was at work among them just as it was among the Jewish believers. His arguments were not merely theoretical; they were based on his personal experiences with Gentile communities, whom he had seen transformed by the message of Christ. Barnabas's respectful yet firm stance helped sway the council toward a decision that would open the doors of the Church to people from all nations without imposing unnecessary burdens. His diplomatic efforts at the Council of Jerusalem were instrumental in shaping the future of Christianity, establishing a foundation for an inclusive Church that welcomed all who believed in Christ, regardless of cultural or religious background.

Barnabas's diplomatic skills were not confined to formal councils; they were evident in his personal relationships within the Church as well. His friendship and partnership with Paul reveal a dynamic marked by mutual respect, even amid differing perspectives. Though they eventually parted ways over a disagreement regarding John Mark, their separation did not diminish the respect they held for each other's work. Barnabas's approach to this disagreement reflects his understanding of diplomacy as a practice rooted in love and mutual respect, one that allows for differences without resorting to animosity. By parting amicably, Barnabas and Paul demonstrated that disagreements could be handled with grace, allowing each to continue their work in a way that honored their respective callings.

Barnabas's diplomatic approach also extended to his relationship with the Jewish Christians in Jerusalem. Though he supported the inclusion of Gentiles, Barnabas maintained strong ties with the Jewish Christian community, respecting their traditions and understanding the value of their heritage. His ability to move between these groups with ease shows a flexibility that was rare among early Church leaders, a willingness to engage with different perspectives without compromising his convictions. Barnabas's respect for Jewish customs did not conflict with his support for Gentile inclusion; rather, it highlighted his commitment to a faith that embraced diversity without abandoning its roots.

In addition to promoting unity within the Church, Barnabas's diplomacy had a wider impact, fostering a spirit of reconciliation and inclusivity that would extend beyond his lifetime. His efforts to bridge divides within the Church helped create a model for handling theological and cultural differences that would influence Christian communities for centuries to come. Barnabas demonstrated that the Church could hold to its core teachings while remaining open to new expressions of faith, a balance that allowed it to grow and adapt in a rapidly changing world. His legacy as a diplomat of faith reflects an understanding that unity in the Church is not achieved through rigid conformity but through a shared commitment to Christ and a willingness to embrace others in love.

Barnabas's diplomacy also serves as a reminder of the importance of humility in Christian leadership. His approach was not marked by arrogance or a desire to dominate others; instead, he listened, respected, and sought to understand different perspectives. This humility enabled him to engage with people from all backgrounds, making him a trusted figure within the Church and a respected voice in debates. Barnabas's humility allowed him to remain open to new ideas and to recognize the work of the Holy Spirit in unexpected places. His diplomatic approach teaches that effective leadership in the Church requires a willingness to learn, to listen, and to prioritize the well-being of the community over personal pride or ambition.

The influence of Barnabas's diplomacy can be seen in the ecumenical efforts of the Church throughout history. His example has inspired countless efforts to foster unity among diverse Christian traditions, encouraging believers to work together in spite of theological or cultural differences. In Barnabas, the Church finds a model for dialogue, one that values understanding and respect over divisiveness. His life reminds Christians that faith can be a force for reconciliation, that differences need not lead to division, and that the Church's strength lies in its ability to bring people together in love.

In the modern Church, Barnabas's legacy as a diplomat of faith remains highly relevant. His approach to unity in diversity offers a framework for addressing the challenges faced by Christian communities in a globalized world. As the Church continues to grow and evolve, it encounters new cultures, beliefs, and practices that test its ability to remain united. Barnabas's life encourages Christians to approach these differences with a spirit of diplomacy, to seek common ground, and to work for unity while respecting the richness of diversity. His example calls the Church to embrace a vision of faith that is expansive, resilient, and able to navigate the complexities of a world that is both interconnected and deeply diverse.

Through his role as a diplomat, Barnabas demonstrated that faith is not only a matter of belief but also a commitment to building relationships, to understanding others, and to fostering harmony within the community of believers. His life invites Christians to reflect on the ways they can contribute to unity within the Church, to consider how they can act as peacemakers, bridge-builders, and advocates for reconciliation. Barnabas's legacy challenges believers to prioritize relationships over differences, to see each other as members of a single body united in Christ.

In his role as a diplomat of faith, Barnabas left a legacy that speaks to the heart of Christian discipleship. His life is a testament to the power of humility, the importance of listening, and the strength found in unity. Barnabas's approach to leadership was one of service, a commitment to the well-being of the Church that transcended personal ambition or ideological rigidity. His life teaches that true faith is not divisive but unifying, not rigid but open, and always oriented toward the love and harmony that are central to the Gospel message.

As Christians look to the future, Barnabas's example offers a guiding light, a reminder that the Church is strongest when it stands together, united in faith and committed to love. His legacy as a diplomat of faith invites believers to embrace a vision of the Church that celebrates diversity, fosters reconciliation, and works tirelessly for the unity that Christ Himself prayed for. Through his life, Barnabas continues to inspire Christians to pursue peace, to build bridges, and to embody the love of God in their relationships with others. His legacy endures as a call to live out a faith that unites, heals, and brings hope to a divided world.

Chapter 16
Exemplary Virtues

Throughout the life of Barnabas, we encounter a man whose character embodied the core virtues of the Christian faith. Barnabas's story is marked not by grand displays of power or authority, but by a quiet strength built upon compassion, humility, generosity, and patience. These virtues guided his interactions, shaped his ministry, and left an enduring impact on the early Church. Barnabas's example serves as a reminder that true greatness in the Christian life is measured not by fame or influence but by the integrity of one's character and the depth of one's love for others.

Among Barnabas's most notable virtues was his deep compassion, a quality that shaped his relationships and decisions from the very beginning of his ministry. Known as the "son of encouragement," Barnabas had an extraordinary ability to empathize with others, to see their struggles, and to offer support without judgment. His compassion was evident in his relationship with Paul, whom he introduced to the apostles despite Paul's history as a persecutor of Christians. Rather than letting fear or prejudice cloud his judgment, Barnabas chose to see the potential for transformation in Paul, extending a welcome that would change the course of Christian history. This act of compassion underscores Barnabas's belief in the power of grace, a faith that saw past a person's past mistakes and embraced the possibility of redemption.

Barnabas's compassion was not limited to those close to him; it extended to entire communities, particularly the Gentiles who were newly entering the Christian faith. When he saw the Spirit of God at work among Gentile converts in Antioch, Barnabas responded with joy and encouragement rather than skepticism or resistance. He welcomed them into the faith with open arms, understanding that compassion called for inclusion and acceptance. His willingness to embrace people from all backgrounds, even when it meant challenging traditional boundaries, reflects a love that reached beyond cultural and religious divides. For Barnabas, compassion was not merely a personal virtue; it was the foundation of his approach to ministry, a way of embodying the inclusive love of Christ.

Another hallmark of Barnabas's character was his humility. Unlike many leaders who seek recognition and prestige, Barnabas consistently placed the needs of others before his own. When he began his missionary journeys with Paul, Barnabas was the more experienced of the two, yet he willingly allowed Paul to take the spotlight as his talents and influence grew. This humility was not a sign of weakness, but of a profound strength rooted in selflessness. Barnabas understood that true leadership in the Christian faith was not about seeking glory but about serving others, even if it meant stepping back to let others shine. His humility reflected his devotion to God, a devotion that valued the advancement of the Gospel over personal recognition.

This humility also extended to his work within the early Christian community, where he acted as a bridge between different factions without asserting his own authority. At the Council of Jerusalem, Barnabas played a critical role in advocating for the inclusion of Gentiles, yet he did so without seeking credit or acclaim. His focus was always on the unity of the Church and the well-being of others, rather than on his own reputation or status. Barnabas's humility allowed him to serve as a peacemaker, a role that required him to put aside personal pride and to seek the good of the community above all else. His actions reveal a leader whose confidence was not in his own abilities but in God's wisdom and grace.

Generosity was another defining virtue in Barnabas's life. One of the earliest acts attributed to him in the Book of Acts is his decision to sell his land and give the proceeds to the apostles, providing for the needs of the community. This act of generosity was more than a material contribution; it was a profound statement of faith and commitment to the Christian community. By relinquishing his own possessions, Barnabas demonstrated his belief that true wealth lay not in material gain but in spiritual solidarity. His generosity inspired others in the early Church to adopt a similar approach, fostering a sense of unity and mutual support that became a hallmark of Christian life. This generosity was not merely financial but extended to his time, energy, and emotional investment in others, revealing a man who gave of himself freely and without reservation.

Barnabas's patience was equally remarkable, evident in his dealings with people who others might have written off. His mentorship of John Mark, despite the young man's earlier failures, reflects a patience born of deep faith in God's transformative power. When John Mark abandoned the mission during an early journey, Paul viewed his departure as an act of weakness or unreliability. But Barnabas, who understood the complexities of growth and faith, saw in John Mark a young man who deserved a second chance. By taking him under his wing and offering him guidance, Barnabas demonstrated a patience that valued long-term development over immediate results. His approach to John Mark reveals a leader who was not quick to judge but who believed in nurturing the potential within each person, no matter how many setbacks they faced.

This patience extended to his broader mission work, where he encountered frequent resistance, misunderstanding, and even hostility. As a missionary, Barnabas faced challenges that tested his resolve, yet he remained steadfast in his commitment to spreading the Gospel. His patience was not passive endurance but an active trust in God's timing and purpose. He understood that faith was a journey, both for himself and for those he encountered, and he approached this journey with a calm and steady resolve. Barnabas's patience in the face of adversity allowed him to persevere without bitterness, reflecting a soul anchored in the peace of God.

Barnabas's integrity was yet another virtue that distinguished him as a leader in the early Church. He was a man whose actions consistently aligned with his beliefs, a quality that earned him the respect of those around him. His integrity was evident in his dedication to the principles of the Gospel, even when it required him to stand against popular opinion or to make personal sacrifices. His unwavering commitment to the inclusion of Gentiles in the Christian faith, despite resistance from some Jewish Christians, reveals a man who valued truth over convenience. For Barnabas, integrity meant remaining true to the teachings of Christ, even when it led to conflict or required difficult choices.

This integrity was closely tied to his courage, a virtue that enabled him to face challenges with grace and conviction. Barnabas's courage was not loud or boastful; it was a quiet strength that allowed him to confront adversity without losing his faith or his sense of purpose. Whether standing alongside Paul in the face of opposition, advocating for Gentile inclusion, or enduring personal hardships, Barnabas displayed a courage that was deeply rooted in his trust in God. His courage was a reflection of his faith, a belief that God's purpose would prevail despite the obstacles he encountered. Through his example, Barnabas showed that courage in the Christian life is not about seeking conflict but about standing firm in one's convictions with humility and grace.

Barnabas's exemplary virtues—compassion, humility, generosity, patience, integrity, and courage—formed the foundation of his leadership and his influence within the early Church. These qualities were not simply personal traits but were deeply intertwined with his spirituality, shaped by his relationship with God and his commitment to the teachings of Christ. Through his actions, Barnabas revealed a faith that was both practical and profound, a faith that found expression in everyday acts of kindness, support, and sacrifice. His life stands as a testament to the idea that true discipleship is not about grand gestures but about the quiet, steady work of living out the Gospel in all aspects of one's life.

The virtues of Barnabas offer a model for Christian living that transcends time, inviting believers to cultivate a faith that is rooted in love, service, and humility. His example challenges Christians to look beyond external accomplishments and to focus instead on the development of character, to seek not personal glory but the well-being of others. Barnabas's life reminds believers that the truest measure of faith is found in how one treats others, in the willingness to forgive, to give, and to guide without expectation of reward.

In reflecting on the life of Barnabas, Christians are called to consider how they might embody these virtues in their own lives. His example encourages believers to approach others with compassion, to serve with humility, and to remain patient in the face of challenges. Barnabas's life teaches that faith is not simply a matter of belief but a way of living, a commitment to embodying the love of Christ in all interactions. His virtues reveal the beauty and strength of a life lived in service to God and to others, a life that continues to inspire and guide believers toward a deeper understanding of what it means to follow Christ.

Through his exemplary virtues, Barnabas left an indelible mark on the early Church, not through power or authority but through the quiet, transformative strength of his character. His legacy calls believers to pursue a path of virtue, to cultivate a heart that seeks the good of others and remains true to the teachings of Christ. In Barnabas, the Church finds a model of discipleship that is humble, compassionate, and courageous, a reminder that the greatest impact comes not from self-interest but from a life dedicated to the service of God and humanity. His life continues to inspire Christians to live with integrity, to love without condition, and to walk humbly with God.

Chapter 17
Persecution and Exile

In the journey of Barnabas, a faithful disciple and unwavering advocate of the Gospel, moments of persecution and exile were defining features. His life was not one of comfort or ease; rather, it was marked by trials that tested his devotion, resilience, and commitment to the mission of Christ. These episodes of hardship underscore Barnabas's courage, revealing a faith that held firm even when confronted by the forces of opposition. As a man driven by his love for God and the message of Christ, Barnabas's encounters with persecution and exile illustrate his profound resilience and the inner strength that carried him through the darkest times.

As one of the earliest apostles, Barnabas faced the reality that the path he chose would not be easy. The world he preached to was often hostile to the message of Christ, particularly as this message challenged established religious, cultural, and political systems. In a society where allegiance to tradition and conformity to social norms were expected, the radical message of the Gospel—emphasizing equality, forgiveness, and devotion to God over adherence to societal rules—sparked resistance. Barnabas knew that his dedication to the Gospel could lead to rejection, alienation, and even violence, yet he pressed forward, motivated by an unshakable conviction in the truth he proclaimed.

The hostility faced by Barnabas was most intense within Jewish communities that regarded Christianity with suspicion and disdain. Though he himself was a Levite, Barnabas's embrace of Christ as the Messiah placed him at odds with the traditional beliefs of his Jewish heritage. His work among the Gentiles, especially his efforts to integrate them into the Christian faith without requiring adherence to Jewish customs, was seen by some as a betrayal of his roots. This tension came to a head as Barnabas traveled and preached in regions where Jewish leaders held considerable influence. For many, his teachings were not only unorthodox but heretical—a direct challenge to the religious identity and traditions they cherished.

The persecution Barnabas encountered was not only verbal or ideological; it was also physical and personal. According to early accounts and tradition, Barnabas endured multiple confrontations, suffering at the hands of those who saw him as a threat to their way of life. His willingness to bear these hardships without retaliation reflects a deep commitment to Christ's teachings on love and forgiveness. Barnabas understood that his mission was not to win arguments or defeat enemies but to bear witness to the transformative power of the Gospel. This meant that, even in the face of hostility, he was called to respond with patience, humility, and resilience, allowing his actions to speak of God's love rather than engaging in conflict.

One of the most significant episodes of Barnabas's persecution occurred during his later missionary work in his homeland of Cyprus. While details of this period are scarce, early traditions suggest that Barnabas's return to Cyprus was met with fierce opposition from local authorities and religious leaders. This opposition was likely intensified by his success in spreading the Gospel, which threatened the established religious structures. His presence on the island became a point of contention, a challenge to the social and religious order. Some accounts indicate that Barnabas was eventually forced into a form of exile, cast out of certain regions where his message was deemed too disruptive. Yet, despite this rejection, he remained steadfast, choosing to continue his work wherever he was welcomed.

Exile, in Barnabas's life, was not merely a geographic separation but an experience that deepened his faith and strengthened his resolve. In leaving behind familiar places and communities, Barnabas encountered a new level of spiritual dependence on God. His exile became a period of inner reflection and renewal, a time when he could draw closer to the Divine and renew his commitment to the mission that had led him to this path. For Barnabas, exile was not a defeat but an opportunity to reaffirm his dedication, to find peace in solitude, and to experience the sustaining presence of God even in isolation. This period of separation allowed him to become even more attuned to the voice of the Spirit, preparing him for the next steps in his journey.

Barnabas's experiences of persecution and exile also served as a source of strength for the early Christian communities he ministered to. His willingness to endure hardship for the sake of the Gospel became a powerful testimony to the resilience and commitment that defined Christian discipleship. In a time when believers often faced hostility and rejection, Barnabas's life served as a beacon of hope, reminding them that faith was worth any sacrifice. His perseverance inspired others to stand firm, to trust in God's provision, and to remain faithful even when the world seemed against them. Barnabas's courage under persecution offered a model for countless Christians who would later face similar challenges, showing them that they, too, could find strength in their relationship with God.

The legacy of Barnabas's endurance is not limited to his personal story; it also resonates within the broader narrative of early Christian resilience. His life reflects the strength found in community, the support that believers offered one another as they navigated a world often hostile to their faith. Barnabas's experiences of exile and persecution became part of the shared memory of the Church, an example that helped shape the identity of Christian communities. In Barnabas, they saw a leader who had endured hardship with grace and integrity, a reminder that they were not alone in their struggles. His story became a symbol of the steadfastness that would come to define the Christian Church, a strength that would carry it through centuries of trials.

The persecution and exile faced by Barnabas also reflect the transformative power of suffering within the Christian life.

For Barnabas, hardship was not a deterrent but a means of drawing closer to God, of finding purpose and peace even in the midst of adversity. His experiences taught him that suffering, when embraced with faith, could become a path to deeper understanding and spiritual growth. This perspective on suffering was not unique to Barnabas but was a foundational aspect of early Christian spirituality, a belief that trials and hardships could bring one closer to God. Barnabas's life exemplified this belief, showing that even the harshest experiences could be met with grace and trust.

In modern times, Barnabas's experiences of persecution and exile continue to resonate with Christians who face similar challenges. His story serves as an encouragement to those who encounter opposition for their beliefs, reminding them that faith can endure even in the most difficult circumstances. His life invites believers to see persecution not as a punishment but as a means of bearing witness to the transformative power of the Gospel. Through his example, Barnabas teaches that faith is not a shield from suffering but a source of strength that allows one to endure it with grace.

The legacy of Barnabas's perseverance also speaks to the role of community in the Christian life. His ability to endure hardship was strengthened by the support of his fellow believers, by the unity and love that defined the early Church. Barnabas's story encourages modern Christians to cultivate communities of mutual support, to walk alongside one another in times of trial, and to find strength in shared faith. His life reminds the Church that unity and compassion are essential for enduring persecution, that believers are called to stand together in the face of adversity.

Through his experiences of persecution and exile, Barnabas left a legacy that continues to inspire believers to pursue a faith that is both courageous and compassionate. His life teaches that the path of discipleship is not always easy, but it is always worthwhile. In Barnabas, we see a man who accepted the cost of his convictions, who found peace even in exile, and who remained faithful to the end. His story is a testament to the power of faith to overcome hardship, a reminder that the journey of faith is one of resilience, hope, and unwavering trust in God.

Barnabas's legacy as a persecuted yet unbroken apostle invites Christians to consider their own responses to hardship. His life calls believers to embrace a faith that is steadfast, a faith that finds strength in God rather than in worldly security. In a world where adversity is often seen as a failure or a punishment, Barnabas's story offers a different perspective, one that sees suffering as an opportunity to grow closer to God, to deepen one's commitment, and to bear witness to the Gospel's transformative power.

In the end, Barnabas's experiences of persecution and exile reveal a life marked by courage, resilience, and an unbreakable faith. His legacy endures as a beacon of hope for those who face opposition, a reminder that true discipleship requires both strength and compassion. Through his life, Barnabas teaches that faith is a journey that often leads through hardship but always leads to God. His example encourages believers to stand firm, to find peace in the midst of trials, and to embrace a faith that endures, no matter the cost.

Chapter 18
Tireless Evangelist

Barnabas, known for his compassion and resilience, was also a tireless evangelist whose dedication to spreading the Gospel knew no bounds. His commitment to evangelism extended across regions, cultures, and communities, and he remained steadfast in his mission despite numerous obstacles. For Barnabas, sharing the message of Christ was not merely an obligation; it was a calling rooted in his profound faith and love for others. His life as an evangelist reflects the depth of his devotion and a zeal that inspired countless others to follow in his footsteps.

Barnabas's journey as an evangelist began within the early Christian community in Jerusalem, where he was known as a man "full of the Holy Spirit and faith." He was drawn to the teachings of Christ, recognizing in them the fulfillment of his Jewish heritage and the beginning of a new covenant. His initial decision to sell his property and donate the proceeds to support the community was not just an act of generosity but an early indication of his commitment to the Christian cause. From the start, Barnabas was all-in, dedicating both his resources and his life to advancing the Gospel.

His work as an evangelist took on a new dimension when he was sent to Antioch by the Jerusalem apostles to observe the growing community of believers there. Antioch, a diverse and bustling city, had become a focal point for the spread of Christianity, attracting people from various backgrounds and beliefs. When Barnabas arrived, he was overjoyed to see the grace of God at work among the Gentiles. Rather than imposing strictures or seeking to convert them to Judaism first, Barnabas encouraged their new faith and exhorted them to remain true to the Lord with "all their hearts." His approach set the tone for a Gospel that was accessible to all, establishing Antioch as a foundational community in the early Church's missionary movement.

Recognizing the magnitude of the work in Antioch, Barnabas went to Tarsus to find Paul, believing that his zeal and theological insight would benefit the mission. Together, they spent a year in Antioch, preaching, teaching, and organizing the new believers into a cohesive community. The partnership between Barnabas and Paul was instrumental in shaping the Antioch church, which would later become a launching point for their missionary journeys. This period of ministry in Antioch reveals Barnabas's capacity to recognize the gifts in others and his willingness to collaborate for the sake of the Gospel. His work was never about personal recognition but about advancing the message of Christ as effectively as possible.

From Antioch, Barnabas and Paul embarked on what would become their first missionary journey, a trek that took them through Cyprus, Pamphylia, and various cities in Asia Minor. Their mission was marked by boldness, resilience, and an unwavering commitment to share the Gospel, even in the face of opposition. In each city they visited, they preached in synagogues, reaching out first to Jewish communities before turning to the Gentiles. Their message was met with mixed reactions—some were receptive, while others resisted or even resorted to violence. Yet, regardless of the response, Barnabas and Paul pressed on, determined to fulfill their calling as evangelists.

One of the defining moments of their mission occurred in Lystra, where, after healing a man who had been crippled, Barnabas and Paul were mistaken for gods by the local population. The people hailed Barnabas as Zeus and Paul as Hermes, a reflection of the cultural and spiritual differences they often encountered in their journeys. Rather than accepting this mistaken adulation, Barnabas and Paul tore their garments in protest, urging the people to turn to the living God instead. This moment underscores Barnabas's humility and his dedication to the true message of the Gospel. He had no interest in fame or flattery; his sole desire was to lead people to Christ, even if it meant correcting their misconceptions or risking their anger.

Throughout his travels, Barnabas faced frequent opposition, often from those who viewed his message as a threat to their religious or social norms. Despite these challenges, he remained steadfast, exhibiting a resilience that became a hallmark of his evangelistic work. Barnabas understood that sharing the Gospel would not always be met with acceptance and that the path of an evangelist was often one of hardship. Yet his love for God and his compassion for others drove him to continue, even when faced with rejection or hostility. For Barnabas, the message of Christ was worth any sacrifice, a belief that propelled him forward in his mission.

The separation from Paul, though painful, did not diminish Barnabas's evangelistic zeal. When they parted ways over a disagreement regarding John Mark, Barnabas continued his mission, taking John Mark with him and returning to Cyprus. This choice reflected Barnabas's commitment to nurturing others and his dedication to the Gospel. His willingness to give John Mark a second chance, even at the cost of his partnership with Paul, underscores his belief in the transformative power of the Gospel and the importance of mentorship within the mission field. Barnabas saw in John Mark a fellow evangelist whose potential could be cultivated, and he was willing to invest in him for the sake of the work they were called to do.

The decision to return to Cyprus, his homeland, was also significant. By bringing the Gospel to his own people, Barnabas demonstrated the personal nature of his mission, a reminder that evangelism often begins with those closest to us. His work in Cyprus likely included revisiting earlier converts, encouraging them to remain faithful, and strengthening the young communities he had helped establish. In returning to familiar ground, Barnabas showed that evangelism was not only about expanding the faith but also about sustaining it, about nurturing the seeds that had already been planted. His mission was one of both breadth and depth, encompassing not only the initial act of conversion but also the ongoing work of discipleship.

Barnabas's tireless evangelism left a profound impact on the early Church, setting a standard for missionary work that combined courage with compassion, resilience with humility. His life serves as a model for all who are called to share the Gospel, demonstrating that true evangelism is rooted in love, driven by a desire to bring others to Christ, and sustained by a willingness to endure hardship. For Barnabas, evangelism was not simply about numbers or conversions; it was about building lasting communities of faith, nurturing believers, and expanding the reach of the Gospel in ways that honored the message and spirit of Christ.

In Barnabas's legacy, we see an evangelist whose work transcended cultural and religious boundaries, a man whose heart for others knew no limits. His ability to connect with diverse communities, to speak to both Jews and Gentiles, and to navigate the challenges of cross-cultural ministry reflects his adaptability and openness. Barnabas understood that the Gospel was a message for all people and that evangelism required an approach that was both inclusive and respectful. His life reminds modern believers that sharing the Gospel means meeting people where they are, understanding their context, and finding ways to communicate the message of Christ in ways that resonate with them.

The example of Barnabas as a tireless evangelist continues to inspire Christians to pursue a mission that is both bold and compassionate. His life challenges believers to approach evangelism with humility, to value relationships over numbers, and to remain committed to the long-term growth of faith communities. Barnabas's story invites Christians to see evangelism not as a task to be completed but as a journey of love, one that involves walking alongside others, supporting them in their faith, and remaining patient even in the face of rejection.

In reflecting on Barnabas's life, Christians are reminded that true evangelism is not about coercion or conquest but about sharing the love of Christ in a way that invites, respects, and uplifts others. Barnabas's legacy calls believers to approach evangelism with a heart of service, to see each person as a beloved child of God, and to trust that the Holy Spirit is at work in every encounter. His life teaches that evangelism is not a one-time event but an ongoing commitment to the growth and well-being of the Church.

Through his tireless efforts, Barnabas helped lay the foundations for a Church that would spread across regions, cultures, and generations. His story is a testament to the power of a life fully dedicated to the Gospel, a life that continues to inspire Christians to pursue their mission with love, courage, and unwavering faith. In Barnabas, the Church finds a model of evangelism that is as relevant today as it was in the first century— a model that speaks to the heart of the Gospel and invites believers to share that message with all who are willing to hear.

Chapter 19
Inspired Writer

While Barnabas's legacy as a missionary and mentor is well-documented, his role as a potential contributor to Christian literature is a facet of his life that invites both intrigue and reverence. Known for his wisdom, insight, and dedication to the Gospel, Barnabas may have played a role in shaping early Christian texts, contributing to the theological foundation of the faith. Although no writings are universally accepted as having come directly from his hand, early Christian tradition and apocryphal sources suggest that Barnabas's influence on early Christian thought extended into the realm of sacred literature. His intellectual and spiritual contributions as an inspired writer, whether through direct authorship or through his influence on others, underscore his legacy as a teacher whose wisdom and insights continue to inspire and challenge believers.

One of the most intriguing works associated with Barnabas is the *Epistle of Barnabas*, a text that, while not included in the New Testament canon, offers valuable insight into the theological debates and perspectives of the early Church. The *Epistle of Barnabas*, likely written in the late first or early second century, reflects a theological perspective that emphasizes the contrast between the old covenant of Jewish law and the new covenant brought through Christ. The text provides a window into early Christian thought and the struggle to define a distinct identity that was both rooted in the Jewish tradition and radically transformed by faith in Christ. Scholars debate whether Barnabas was the author of this epistle or whether it was attributed to him by later writers who wished to lend authority to the work. Regardless of authorship, the text echoes themes that resonate with Barnabas's known character and ministry—particularly his desire to bring unity and clarity to the Christian message.

The *Epistle of Barnabas* is characterized by a firm rejection of certain Jewish practices and a call to view the Old Testament scriptures through a Christ-centered lens. This approach aligns with Barnabas's known mission to embrace Gentile converts and to advocate for a faith that did not impose traditional Jewish customs on new believers. The epistle uses allegorical interpretations of scripture, often reinterpreting Jewish symbols and laws as metaphors for Christian teachings. This emphasis on symbolism and deeper spiritual meaning reflects a mystical dimension to Barnabas's thought, showing him to be not only a practical leader but also a visionary thinker. In this light, the *Epistle of Barnabas* can be seen as an attempt to guide early Christians toward a theological understanding that reconciles their Jewish heritage with their new identity in Christ.

The text also emphasizes the theme of spiritual renewal, a concept that Barnabas championed in his work as a missionary and mentor. For Barnabas, the transformation brought by Christ was not merely an external change but a profound inner rebirth that reoriented one's entire life. This idea of renewal, reflected in the *Epistle of Barnabas*, speaks to the heart of his ministry and his belief in the transformative power of the Gospel. Through his writings, Barnabas sought to encourage believers to live in accordance with the teachings of Christ, to forsake the "old self" and embrace a new life rooted in love, faith, and service. This message of renewal resonated with early Christian communities who sought to distinguish themselves from their former lives and embrace a radical, Christ-centered way of being.

In addition to the *Epistle of Barnabas*, early Christian tradition attributes other writings to him, though none have been verified with certainty. Some scholars speculate that Barnabas may have contributed to the shaping of the teachings in the Gospel of Mark, given his close relationship with John Mark, whom tradition holds as the author of this canonical Gospel. If Barnabas did indeed influence John Mark's writing, his impact on Christian literature would be even greater, contributing to one of the four foundational texts of the New Testament. Through his mentorship, Barnabas would have imparted his own experiences and theological insights to John Mark, who may have incorporated these ideas into his Gospel narrative. This indirect influence highlights the enduring legacy of Barnabas's teaching and his role as a guide in the transmission of the Christian message.

Barnabas's role as an inspired writer also extends to the broader oral tradition within the early Church. In a time when few believers had access to written texts, oral teaching was the primary means by which the Gospel was spread and preserved. Barnabas, known for his eloquence and wisdom, was a key figure in this tradition, passing on the teachings of Christ through his preaching and storytelling. His ability to communicate complex theological ideas in a way that resonated with diverse audiences suggests a man who understood the power of words and the importance of clarity in sharing the faith. As a preacher, Barnabas likely influenced countless believers, embedding the core teachings of Christ within the hearts and minds of those he encountered.

Beyond his own writings or potential contributions to the texts of others, Barnabas's influence on Christian literature can also be seen in the theological themes that his life exemplified—grace, inclusivity, unity, and renewal. These themes, embodied by Barnabas in both his words and actions, shaped the development of early Christian theology and served as foundational concepts that would recur throughout Christian writings. The emphasis on a faith open to all, regardless of cultural or religious background, reflects Barnabas's impact on the Church's understanding of itself as a community that transcends human divisions. His life and teachings underscored the transformative nature of the Gospel, a message that invites all people to participate in the redemptive work of Christ.

The possibility of Barnabas as an inspired writer also sheds light on the concept of spiritual inspiration within the early Church. For early believers, inspiration was not limited to written words but was a lived experience that encompassed all aspects of one's ministry and interactions with others. Barnabas, filled with the Holy Spirit, exemplified a life of inspired action, where every teaching, every act of compassion, and every word of encouragement was a reflection of the divine message he carried within him. His writings, whether directly or indirectly, were an extension of this inspired life, a means of communicating the Gospel in a form that would endure beyond his lifetime. Through his example, Barnabas shows that inspiration is not merely about producing texts but about embodying the values and truths of the faith in every aspect of one's life.

Barnabas's legacy as an inspired writer, teacher, and evangelist continues to shape the Christian tradition, inviting believers to consider how they, too, might contribute to the ongoing story of the faith. His life challenges Christians to approach scripture with both reverence and openness, to seek deeper meanings within the teachings of Christ, and to embrace the call to share these insights with others. Barnabas's example encourages believers to cultivate a life of spiritual inspiration, one that is rooted in love for God and dedication to the community of faith.

For the early Church, Barnabas represented a bridge between the written word and the lived experience of faith. His teachings and actions demonstrated that the Gospel was not confined to texts but was a vibrant, transformative reality that could be encountered in every aspect of life. His legacy as an inspired writer invites modern believers to engage with scripture not only as a historical document but as a living message, one that speaks to the heart of each individual and calls them to a deeper relationship with God.

Barnabas's role in the formation of Christian thought highlights the importance of mentorship, storytelling, and the transmission of wisdom through both written and spoken word.

His life teaches that the most enduring legacy is not necessarily found in physical texts but in the lives and hearts of those who carry on the teachings. In this way, Barnabas's influence is as much spiritual as it is literary, a reminder that each believer is a living testament to the faith and that every act of love, kindness, and wisdom contributes to the unfolding story of the Gospel.

As Christians reflect on Barnabas's legacy as an inspired writer, they are reminded of the power of words to shape faith, to build community, and to offer hope. His life invites believers to see themselves as stewards of this message, called to pass on the truths of the faith with humility, compassion, and dedication. Through his example, Barnabas encourages each Christian to be a bearer of the Word, to live in a way that reflects the love of Christ, and to contribute to the ongoing narrative of redemption that began with the apostles and continues in the lives of believers today.

In the end, Barnabas's role as an inspired writer and teacher underscores his dedication to a faith that was both intellectually rich and spiritually profound. His contributions to early Christian thought, whether through direct writings or his influence on others, reflect a man who understood the power of words to change lives. His legacy invites Christians to seek a faith that is deeply rooted in scripture, yet open to the fresh inspiration of the Spirit, a faith that is both timeless and alive. Through his life, Barnabas left a legacy that continues to inspire believers to approach their faith with curiosity, dedication, and a commitment to sharing the message of Christ with all who seek it.

Chapter 20
Oral Tradition and Spiritual Legacy

The legacy of Barnabas, while deeply rooted in the early writings and history of the Christian faith, also lives on through the oral traditions and stories that emerged around his life and mission. In the early Church, long before the canon of scripture was fully established, the teachings and acts of the apostles were preserved primarily through spoken word. Barnabas's life, full of courage, compassion, and commitment to spreading the Gospel, became a part of this living tradition—a legacy carried forward by those who heard his story, shared his teachings, and sought to emulate his faith. Through these oral traditions, Barnabas's influence grew, and his spirit continued to shape and inspire the Christian community, creating a foundation that would support the Church for centuries to come.

The oral tradition surrounding Barnabas was rich and multifaceted, encompassing stories of his missionary journeys, his encounters with diverse communities, and his acts of kindness and courage. In a time when literacy was rare and written texts were not widely accessible, oral storytelling was the lifeblood of the Church, a means of preserving the faith and passing it down from generation to generation. Barnabas, known for his humility and encouragement, was remembered not only as an apostle but as a beloved figure whose life served as a testament to the power of the Gospel. His story was shared among believers, inspiring them to persevere, to welcome outsiders, and to live with the same spirit of generosity and courage.

Among the stories passed down orally were accounts of Barnabas's travels and the miraculous events that accompanied his mission. His journey to Antioch, where he welcomed Gentile converts with joy, became a defining moment in the narrative of the early Church's expansion beyond its Jewish roots. This story, recounted and retold in Christian communities, reinforced the message that the Gospel was meant for all people, a message that resonated with believers from diverse backgrounds. Through this oral tradition, Barnabas was celebrated as a bridge-builder, a man who embraced inclusivity and recognized the work of the Holy Spirit in every person, regardless of their cultural or religious background.

Another aspect of Barnabas's oral legacy centered on his friendship and partnership with Paul. Their relationship, marked by both unity and eventual separation, became a story that highlighted the importance of reconciliation and respect within the Church. Believers shared tales of Barnabas's unwavering support for Paul when he first sought acceptance among the apostles, recounting how Barnabas had advocated for Paul despite his past as a persecutor. This story of loyalty and forgiveness became part of the Church's narrative, serving as a reminder that the Christian community was founded on grace and mutual support. Even their eventual disagreement over John Mark, which led to their parting ways, was told as a lesson in the importance of diversity within the body of Christ. Barnabas's decision to stand by John Mark, despite Paul's reluctance, became an emblem of his compassion and patience, qualities that would be celebrated in the Church's oral tradition.

The stories of Barnabas also included accounts of his encounters with hardship and persecution, moments that underscored his resilience and unwavering faith. These accounts, shared among believers facing their own trials, offered hope and strength. The story of Barnabas's persecution in Cyprus, where he ultimately gave his life for the Gospel, became a narrative of martyrdom that resonated deeply with early Christians. His willingness to suffer and even die for his faith served as an example of ultimate devotion, inspiring others to remain steadfast in the face of adversity. Through these stories, Barnabas's courage and dedication were kept alive, reminding believers that the path of discipleship often required sacrifice but was always sustained by the promise of God's presence.

The oral traditions about Barnabas also encompassed his teachings, his words of encouragement, and his emphasis on unity and compassion. Known as the "son of encouragement," Barnabas's legacy included countless stories of how he uplifted and inspired those around him. Whether in private conversations, sermons, or public gatherings, Barnabas was remembered as a man whose words brought comfort, strength, and hope. His teachings on forgiveness, inclusivity, and the transformative power of faith were shared and passed down, shaping the values of early Christian communities. Through these stories, Barnabas's voice continued to guide believers, helping them to navigate their own spiritual journeys and to foster communities rooted in love and mutual support.

One of the most profound aspects of Barnabas's spiritual legacy is the way in which his life embodied the teachings of Christ, offering a living example of the Gospel in action. In an era when written scripture was not yet fully accessible, the example of Barnabas served as a tangible representation of Christian virtues. His generosity, exemplified by his decision to sell his land and give the proceeds to the apostles, became a story that highlighted the importance of selflessness and communal care. This act, recounted and celebrated within the Church, inspired other believers to embrace a spirit of generosity, to see their possessions as gifts to be shared rather than hoarded. Barnabas's life became a parable of Christ's teaching on self-sacrifice and love for others, a story that encouraged believers to live with open hearts and hands.

The oral tradition surrounding Barnabas also preserved his emphasis on reconciliation and unity, values that were essential to the cohesion of the early Church. His role in advocating for Gentile inclusion and his efforts to mediate conflicts within the community were remembered as acts of wisdom and compassion. These stories reinforced the idea that the Church was a place of belonging for all people, a community that transcended cultural and religious divisions. Barnabas's example reminded believers that the Gospel called for a unity that honored diversity, a unity built on respect and mutual support rather than conformity. His legacy encouraged Christians to seek reconciliation, to embrace differences, and to work together for the common good.

As the Church grew and evolved, the stories of Barnabas continued to inspire believers to live with integrity, courage, and compassion. His life, preserved through oral tradition, became part of the spiritual heritage of the Church, a source of wisdom and encouragement for those who came after him. Barnabas's story was not simply a historical account; it was a narrative that conveyed timeless truths, a story that invited each believer to reflect on their own faith and their role within the community of Christ. His example encouraged Christians to see themselves as part of a larger story, to recognize that their actions, like his, could leave a lasting impact on those around them.

The legacy of Barnabas in the oral tradition also highlights the power of storytelling within the Christian faith. His life demonstrates that faith is not only a set of doctrines but a lived experience, a journey that is best understood through the sharing of stories. Through the tales of his courage, compassion, and perseverance, Barnabas's legacy became a living tradition, a source of inspiration that was passed from one generation to the next. This oral tradition reminded believers that each of their lives was a part of the ongoing story of the Gospel, that their own acts of kindness, resilience, and faith could become part of the spiritual heritage they would leave behind.

In the modern Church, the legacy of Barnabas as preserved through oral tradition continues to inspire believers to live lives of faith and compassion. His example calls Christians to embrace their own spiritual journey, to share their stories of faith, and to recognize the ways in which their lives contribute to the larger narrative of the Church. Barnabas's life encourages believers to see themselves as part of a spiritual lineage, a lineage that stretches back to the apostles and is enriched by each generation's contributions. His legacy reminds the Church that faith is not only preserved through texts but through the lives of those who embody its teachings, through the stories they share and the values they uphold.

Through the oral tradition and spiritual legacy of Barnabas, we see a man whose life was a testament to the power of the Gospel to transform individuals and communities. His story, passed down through generations, continues to inspire believers to pursue a faith that is rooted in love, dedicated to unity, and open to all people. Barnabas's legacy invites each Christian to consider how they, too, might contribute to the story of the faith, how their own lives might reflect the virtues and values that he exemplified. His life teaches that faith is not merely a matter of words but a way of being, a path of discipleship that calls each believer to live with courage, generosity, and a spirit of encouragement.

In the end, Barnabas's oral legacy is a reminder that each believer's story has the power to shape and inspire the Church. His life invites us to carry forward the message of Christ not only through written texts but through the way we live, love, and share our faith with others. Barnabas's legacy as preserved in oral tradition continues to be a light for the Church, guiding believers toward a faith that is alive, active, and deeply connected to the enduring story of the Gospel. Through his example, Christians are called to become living witnesses of their faith, to pass on their own spiritual legacy, and to contribute to the ongoing story of God's love in the world.

Chapter 21
Disciple of Jesus

In exploring the life of Barnabas, a compelling question arises about his relationship to Jesus and the ways in which he may have been connected to the direct teachings of Christ. Though Barnabas is introduced later in the New Testament, particularly in the Book of Acts, his actions, character, and influence strongly reflect the values and teachings central to the ministry of Jesus. Barnabas's legacy reveals not only a deep commitment to the Gospel but also the unmistakable marks of a life transformed by the message and spirit of Christ.

While no historical evidence conclusively ties Barnabas to the Twelve Apostles or to direct encounters with Jesus during His ministry, early Christian tradition and certain historical records suggest that Barnabas might have been one of the seventy disciples sent by Jesus to spread His teachings. This idea is compelling for understanding the depth of Barnabas's commitment, as it would mean that he was not only a follower of Jesus's teachings but a man who had encountered them firsthand. Being among the seventy would have placed him in a position of spiritual influence and responsibility, charged with carrying forward the message of repentance, healing, and hope to those he encountered. This formative experience would have cemented his dedication to Christ and shaped his later ministry as one of the early Church's most prominent figures.

Barnabas's work as a disciple is perhaps most evident in his embodiment of Christ-like virtues, particularly his compassion, humility, and unyielding dedication to unity among believers. Throughout his ministry, Barnabas's actions reflected the essence of Jesus's command to "love one another" and to show mercy and kindness, even in the face of opposition. He demonstrated these qualities repeatedly, welcoming new believers, extending forgiveness to those who had faltered, and bridging divides within the early Christian community. These actions were not only marks of a good man but the very expressions of a disciple who had internalized Christ's teachings on love, reconciliation, and compassion.

One of the central teachings of Jesus that resonated with Barnabas was the call to inclusivity and the expansion of the Kingdom of God to all people. Jesus broke cultural and social barriers by extending His message to Samaritans, Romans, and other marginalized groups. Similarly, Barnabas became known for his acceptance of Gentile believers and his advocacy for their inclusion within the early Church. When he arrived in Antioch and saw the faith and devotion of Gentile converts, he was quick to welcome them into the community, encouraging their new faith without imposing Jewish customs upon them. This open-hearted approach echoed the inclusive nature of Jesus's ministry, revealing Barnabas as a disciple who understood the essence of Christ's message and was determined to live it out.

Barnabas's role in mentoring other leaders, particularly Paul and John Mark, also highlights his status as a disciple of Jesus. Jesus's ministry included nurturing and guiding His apostles, empowering them to carry forward His teachings and to become leaders in their own right. In Barnabas's relationship with Paul, we see a similar spirit of mentorship and encouragement. When others doubted Paul's conversion, it was Barnabas who stood by him, vouching for the authenticity of his faith and helping to integrate him into the Christian community. His support and belief in Paul reflect the trust and patience of a true disciple, someone who had learned from Christ the value of second chances and the importance of nurturing potential in others. Through this mentorship, Barnabas not only supported

Paul's growth but contributed to the foundation of Christian leadership, a testament to his dedication to the mission of Jesus.

Another aspect of Barnabas's life that reflects his discipleship is his commitment to living simply and sharing his resources with the community, an echo of Jesus's teachings on generosity and self-sacrifice. Early in the Book of Acts, Barnabas is described as selling his land and giving the proceeds to the apostles to support the needs of the Christian community. This act of generosity reveals a heart devoted to Christ's command to "store up treasures in heaven" rather than earthly wealth. For Barnabas, following Jesus meant living in a way that prioritized the welfare of others, a life that placed spiritual riches above material gain. His example inspired other believers, fostering a spirit of mutual support and communal care that became one of the defining characteristics of the early Church.

Barnabas's humility, another key quality in his discipleship, is evident in his willingness to take a supportive role, allowing others, like Paul, to take the lead as their own ministries developed. Just as Jesus taught His disciples that "the first shall be last," Barnabas demonstrated a humility that placed the mission above personal recognition. This humility is a mark of a disciple who has internalized the values of Christ, understanding that leadership in the Christian community is about service rather than status. Barnabas's willingness to step back, to support rather than dominate, reflects a faith that is grounded in the teachings of Christ and committed to fostering a community where each person's gifts are celebrated and nurtured.

The theme of reconciliation, central to Jesus's ministry, was also a key part of Barnabas's life and legacy. Jesus taught His disciples to forgive others, to seek unity, and to build bridges of peace. Barnabas's dedication to unity and his efforts to mediate conflicts within the early Church reflect this commitment to reconciliation. His role at the Council of Jerusalem, where he argued for the inclusion of Gentiles without the imposition of Jewish customs, was an act of peacemaking that helped preserve the unity of the Church. Barnabas's efforts to keep the Church united, despite its growing diversity, reveal a disciple who had learned from Jesus the importance of harmony, forgiveness, and the courage to stand for what is just.

In addition to embodying the teachings of Jesus, Barnabas also contributed to the preservation and transmission of these teachings. While he may not have been a direct author of the Gospels, his role in shaping and guiding early Christian leaders, such as Paul and John Mark, would have influenced the way Christ's message was understood and conveyed. Barnabas's life and ministry ensured that the teachings of Jesus were not only preserved in words but were made manifest through actions, creating a living testimony to the power of the Gospel. His life as a disciple was thus both a reflection of Jesus's teachings and a means by which those teachings were carried forward, alive in the hearts and minds of those he inspired.

Barnabas's discipleship was further marked by his resilience in the face of persecution, a quality that mirrored the courage of Jesus. Despite the hardships he encountered, including rejection, opposition, and ultimately martyrdom, Barnabas remained steadfast in his commitment to the Gospel. His willingness to suffer for his faith reveals a heart that was wholly devoted to Christ, a man whose discipleship was not conditional upon comfort or safety but was rooted in a deep and abiding love for the message of Jesus. Barnabas's life challenges modern believers to embrace a discipleship that is not superficial but grounded in a commitment that endures through trials and hardships.

The life of Barnabas as a disciple of Jesus invites believers to consider the depth of their own commitment to Christ. His example calls Christians to a discipleship that is not merely about belief but about transformation, a journey that requires them to embody the teachings of Christ in all aspects of their lives. Through his actions, Barnabas demonstrates that true discipleship is a way of being—a life dedicated to love, service, and unity. His life encourages believers to see themselves not only as followers but as active participants in the mission of Jesus, people called to make a difference in the world through their faith.

In the legacy of Barnabas, we see a disciple whose life reflected the spirit and teachings of Jesus, a man who carried forward the Gospel not only in words but in deeds. His life reminds Christians that discipleship is an invitation to be transformed, to live with courage, compassion, and a heart open to all. Through his example, Barnabas teaches that to be a disciple is to walk in the footsteps of Christ, to embrace a life of humility, generosity, and unwavering faith. His story calls each believer to examine their own journey, to ask themselves how they might live as disciples in a world that needs the message of Christ as much today as it did in the time of Barnabas.

Ultimately, Barnabas's life as a disciple of Jesus is a legacy of faith in action. His journey invites believers to follow Christ not only in belief but in every aspect of their lives, to become living testimonies to the love, hope, and transformation that Jesus brought into the world. Through his discipleship, Barnabas left a legacy that continues to inspire, a legacy that challenges Christians to live with the same courage, compassion, and dedication that he embodied. His life reminds us that the call to discipleship is a call to transformation, a call to become a reflection of Christ's love in the world.

Chapter 22
Leadership in the Church

In the formative years of the early Christian Church, Barnabas emerged as a guiding figure whose leadership style combined humility, inclusivity, and a deep commitment to the teachings of Christ. His leadership extended beyond his missionary journeys; it touched the structure, values, and growth of the Christian community. Unlike the hierarchical or authoritarian models of leadership common in the world around him, Barnabas's approach was rooted in service, mutual support, and an understanding that each member of the community had a role in carrying forward the message of Christ. His role in shaping the early Church reflects a leader who not only inspired through words but laid down an example of how a Christian leader should serve, build, and sustain a faith community.

Barnabas's leadership style can be seen in his ability to recognize and nurture the gifts in others, particularly in Paul, whom he mentored and introduced to the apostles. Following Paul's conversion, Barnabas extended to him an invitation to join the Christian community in a way that was both welcoming and affirming. This act of inclusion went beyond mere acceptance; it involved advocating for Paul, vouching for the sincerity of his transformation, and bringing him into the fold of trusted leaders. This moment exemplifies Barnabas's capacity to see beyond an individual's past, recognizing the potential within each person and encouraging them to grow into their calling. His support for Paul was a turning point for the early Church, demonstrating that its leadership was to be based not on past achievements or social status but on faith, potential, and commitment to the Gospel.

Barnabas's leadership in Antioch provides another powerful example of his role in shaping the early Church. As the first major Christian community to include both Jewish and Gentile believers, Antioch presented unique challenges and opportunities. When the apostles sent Barnabas to observe and nurture this community, he responded not by imposing rigid structures or doctrines but by encouraging the believers to remain true to the teachings of Christ. His leadership in Antioch set a precedent for inclusivity, showing that the Church was not bound by ethnicity, tradition, or social background. By embracing Gentile believers and affirming their place within the Christian community, Barnabas helped establish a vision of the Church as a universal body, one that would extend far beyond the borders of Jerusalem and the Jewish faith.

As a leader, Barnabas demonstrated a rare blend of flexibility and steadfastness. His adaptability allowed him to meet the unique needs of each community he encountered, whether in Jerusalem, Antioch, or Cyprus. Rather than insisting on a one-size-fits-all approach, Barnabas tailored his leadership to the cultural, spiritual, and social contexts of each community, ensuring that the Gospel could be understood and embraced by people from all walks of life. His ability to adapt while remaining committed to the core teachings of Christ reflects a leader who understood that true leadership is about meeting people where they are, helping them grow in their faith without losing sight of the foundational values that define the Christian life.

The Council of Jerusalem offers further insight into Barnabas's leadership and his dedication to unity within the Church. The issue at hand—the question of whether Gentile converts should be required to follow Jewish customs—threatened to divide the Christian community. Barnabas, along with Paul, advocated for a solution that would allow Gentiles to join the Church without the burden of adherence to Jewish laws. His role in this council highlights his wisdom, his courage, and his commitment to an inclusive Church. By seeking a path that would honor both Jewish and Gentile believers, Barnabas modeled a leadership rooted in compassion, compromise, and a profound respect for diversity. His actions at the council reflect a vision of the Church that is united not by uniformity but by a shared faith in Christ, a vision that would shape the future of Christianity.

Barnabas's approach to leadership was also marked by a profound humility and a willingness to place the needs of others above his own. Throughout his ministry, he consistently demonstrated a commitment to service rather than self-promotion. Even as a respected leader, he remained humble, often taking a supporting role and allowing others, like Paul, to rise to prominence. This humility was not a sign of weakness but a reflection of his dedication to the values of Christ, who taught that true greatness lies in serving others. Barnabas's leadership was rooted in a desire to uplift, empower, and encourage those around him, qualities that made him a beloved and trusted figure within the early Church.

His role as a leader also extended to his mentorship of John Mark, a young believer who faced setbacks and challenges in his early ministry. When John Mark abandoned the first missionary journey, Paul viewed him as unreliable, but Barnabas saw potential in him and gave him a second chance. By choosing to mentor John Mark, even at the cost of his partnership with Paul, Barnabas demonstrated that Christian leadership is not about perfection but about nurturing growth and transformation. His decision to support John Mark reflects a leader who believed in the redemptive power of grace, a leader who was willing to invest in others despite their shortcomings. Through this mentorship, Barnabas ensured that the Church would have leaders who understood the value of patience, forgiveness, and perseverance.

In addition to his personal qualities, Barnabas's leadership helped shape the structure and organization of the early Church. As communities of believers grew across different regions, there was a need for leadership that could provide guidance, maintain unity, and ensure that the teachings of Christ were upheld. Barnabas's work in establishing and strengthening these communities laid the groundwork for what would become the broader organizational structure of the Church. His leadership created a framework within which believers could grow, serve, and support one another, fostering a sense of shared mission and purpose. This structure was not hierarchical in nature but was rooted in mutual respect, shared responsibility, and a commitment to the teachings of Christ.

Barnabas's leadership in the early Church also set a standard for future generations of Christian leaders, inspiring them to embrace a model of leadership based on service, humility, and love. His example challenged later Church leaders to reject power for power's sake, to resist the lure of authority and instead focus on building up the community of believers. Barnabas's approach to leadership, marked by inclusivity, flexibility, and an unwavering commitment to unity, became a model that would influence Christian thought and practice for centuries. His life and ministry serve as a reminder that the true strength of the Church lies in its ability to welcome, nurture, and empower each believer, creating a community that reflects the love and compassion of Christ.

In a broader sense, Barnabas's legacy as a leader speaks to the nature of Christian leadership as a whole. His life teaches that to lead within the Church is to be a servant, to seek the good of others, and to approach each task with humility and grace. His leadership challenges modern believers to view their roles within the Church not as positions of power but as opportunities to serve, to uplift, and to guide others in their spiritual journey. Barnabas's example reminds Christians that true leadership is not about personal ambition but about fulfilling the mission of Christ, creating a community where every member is valued, every voice is heard, and every need is met.

Through his leadership, Barnabas left an indelible mark on the Church, shaping its identity and setting a standard for future leaders to follow. His life calls each believer to reflect on their own role within the body of Christ, to consider how they might contribute to the growth, unity, and vitality of the Church. Barnabas's example invites Christians to embrace a leadership that is rooted in love, a leadership that seeks to build bridges, to heal divisions, and to bring others closer to God. His legacy as a leader continues to inspire believers to pursue a path of service, compassion, and unwavering dedication to the Gospel.

In the end, Barnabas's leadership was more than a set of actions; it was an embodiment of the values he held dear. His life as a leader challenges the Church to rise to a higher standard, to cultivate a community that is open, inclusive, and grounded in the teachings of Christ. His example calls believers to lead with humility, to embrace diversity, and to work tirelessly for the unity of the Church. Through his life and legacy, Barnabas teaches that the true measure of leadership is found not in titles or accolades but in the love, support, and inspiration one provides to others. His legacy endures as a reminder that each believer has a role to play in building the Church, a role that calls for humility, faith, and a heart devoted to the mission of Christ.

Chapter 23
Theology and Doctrine

Barnabas's contributions to the early Christian Church went beyond his leadership, mentorship, and missionary work. He played a pivotal role in shaping early Christian theology and doctrine, offering insights that bridged the Jewish tradition with the emerging Christian faith. As the early Church sought to define its beliefs, Barnabas's theological perspective provided a foundation that balanced tradition with innovation, deeply influencing the way early Christians understood the teachings of Jesus. Through his commitment to inclusivity, his understanding of grace, and his respect for the Law's spiritual meaning, Barnabas helped forge a theological path that embraced diversity and encouraged unity within the faith.

Barnabas's background as a Levite from Cyprus provided him with a strong foundation in Jewish teachings, customs, and scripture. This heritage would have shaped his understanding of God's covenant with Israel and the promises fulfilled through Jesus, the Messiah. However, Barnabas's theological vision was not constrained by traditionalism; rather, he saw Jesus's teachings as a revelation that expanded and reinterpreted the Jewish faith. He understood the new covenant in Christ as a fulfillment of the Law and the Prophets, and he sought to articulate a theology that honored Jewish tradition while making space for Gentile believers. This synthesis was essential in helping early Christian communities establish an identity that was distinct yet respectful of its roots.

One of the most significant theological contributions of Barnabas was his perspective on grace and salvation. Barnabas believed that salvation was a gift from God, available to all through faith in Jesus Christ. This stance was revolutionary for the early Church, as it challenged the prevailing belief that adherence to the Mosaic Law was a prerequisite for salvation. Barnabas saw the Law not as a means of earning righteousness but as a guide that pointed to the need for grace and redemption through Christ. His teachings emphasized that salvation could not be earned through human effort but was a result of God's love and mercy, accessible to all who believed. This emphasis on grace helped establish a foundational doctrine within Christianity, one that celebrated God's generosity and offered hope to believers of all backgrounds.

Barnabas's role in advocating for the inclusion of Gentiles without requiring them to adopt Jewish customs also reflects his theological stance on the universality of the Gospel. He believed that the message of Christ was meant for all people, regardless of cultural or religious background. This belief was central to his work in Antioch and later at the Council of Jerusalem, where he argued that Gentile converts should not be burdened with the traditional Jewish requirements. By advocating for a faith that transcended ethnic and cultural boundaries, Barnabas helped shape a theology that emphasized unity in diversity—a vision of the Church as a body that welcomed all who professed faith in Christ. His stance at the council contributed to the doctrinal understanding that faith in Jesus alone was the cornerstone of Christian identity, a doctrine that would become central to the Church's mission and identity.

In addition to his contributions on grace and inclusivity, Barnabas's theological insights extended to the interpretation of scripture. Early Christian theology was characterized by a re-reading of Hebrew scriptures in light of Christ's life and teachings. Barnabas, like many early Christians, believed that the Old Testament contained foreshadowings and prophecies that were fulfilled in Jesus. His approach to scripture was deeply

Christological, viewing the Law and the Prophets as pointing toward the coming Messiah. This perspective encouraged a way of reading scripture that saw continuity between the Old and New Testaments, an interpretative approach that would influence Christian theology for centuries. Barnabas's teachings emphasized that the true meaning of scripture could only be understood through the lens of Christ, inviting believers to see the Old Testament not as a separate covenant but as part of the divine story completed in Jesus.

The *Epistle of Barnabas*, an early Christian text traditionally attributed to Barnabas, although its authorship remains debated, offers further insight into his theological perspectives. This epistle, with its strong emphasis on the symbolic interpretation of scripture, reflects a mystical and allegorical approach that was present in Barnabas's teachings. In the *Epistle of Barnabas*, the author reinterprets various Jewish rituals and laws as symbols that foreshadowed the coming of Christ. For example, the epistle views circumcision not as a physical act but as a metaphor for the transformation of the heart. This allegorical approach shows Barnabas's willingness to go beyond literal interpretations, seeking deeper spiritual meanings that reveal God's purpose and plan in history. His use of symbolism and allegory highlights his role as a teacher who encouraged believers to seek the spiritual truths behind religious practices, fostering a theology that was both profound and accessible.

Barnabas's theological contributions also included his emphasis on community and fellowship as central to the Christian faith. For Barnabas, belief in Christ was not an isolated experience but one that bound believers together in a new kind of family, united by faith and love. His teachings encouraged Christians to view themselves as members of a single body, called to support, care for, and encourage one another. This emphasis on community was reflected in his actions, such as selling his property to support the early Church and advocating for the inclusion of marginalized groups. Barnabas's theology of community helped to shape the early Church's understanding of itself as a fellowship of believers, committed to living out the teachings of Christ in daily life. His vision of a united, inclusive Church provided a model that would inspire Christian communities throughout history.

Furthermore, Barnabas's theology emphasized the transformative nature of faith, a belief that conversion to Christianity was not merely an acceptance of new doctrines but a total renewal of one's heart and mind. He saw baptism as a rite that symbolized this transformation, marking the believer's rebirth into a life of faith, love, and service. This emphasis on inner transformation was central to his message, reflecting his conviction that true discipleship involved a radical change in values, priorities, and actions. Barnabas's teaching on transformation encouraged believers to live in a way that reflected the love of Christ, to let go of selfishness, and to embrace a life dedicated to God and to others. His understanding of conversion as a process of deep, personal change became a key aspect of Christian theology, shaping the Church's teachings on the nature of faith and the life of the believer.

Barnabas's contributions to early Christian theology also included his teachings on peace, reconciliation, and forgiveness. As a mediator and bridge-builder, he emphasized the importance of maintaining harmony within the Church. His theological perspective on forgiveness was not merely theoretical; it was evident in his actions, such as his willingness to give John Mark a second chance despite previous failures. This emphasis on reconciliation reflected a belief in the redemptive power of grace and the importance of extending that grace to others. Barnabas's teachings on forgiveness and peace would influence the Church's understanding of communal life, fostering an environment where believers could grow in faith while supporting one another. His theology emphasized that the Church was a place of healing, where believers could experience God's forgiveness and learn to forgive one another.

The legacy of Barnabas's theology continues to influence Christian thought and practice, providing a foundation for doctrines that emphasize grace, inclusivity, community, and inner transformation. His teachings invite believers to embrace a faith that is both deeply rooted in tradition and open to the Spirit's guidance, a faith that seeks to reconcile rather than divide. Barnabas's theological vision challenges the Church to remain committed to its core values while welcoming diversity, to uphold the teachings of Christ while adapting to the needs of each generation. His contributions remind Christians that theology is not merely an intellectual exercise but a lived reality, one that shapes the way believers understand God, interact with others, and live out their faith in the world.

Barnabas's influence on Christian theology reflects a leader who understood that faith is not static but dynamic, a journey that requires both commitment to tradition and openness to new insights. His teachings on grace, inclusivity, and transformation continue to resonate with believers, offering a framework for a theology that is as relevant today as it was in the early Church. Through his theological insights, Barnabas helped to lay the foundation for a Church that is grounded in love, guided by wisdom, and open to all who seek the truth.

In the end, Barnabas's contributions to theology and doctrine are a testament to his depth of faith and his commitment to the Gospel. His teachings challenge believers to embrace a faith that is both compassionate and courageous, a faith that invites all people into a relationship with God. Through his life and teachings, Barnabas left a legacy that continues to shape the Church, reminding Christians that true theology is a reflection of Christ's love, a love that transcends boundaries, welcomes diversity, and transforms hearts. His example encourages the Church to remain faithful to its calling, to seek wisdom in its teachings, and to live out a theology that embodies the grace and truth of the Gospel.

Chapter 24
Inclusive and Ecumenical Vision

Barnabas, known as the "son of encouragement," not only nurtured individuals in their faith but also pioneered a vision of the Church that was inclusive and ecumenical. His work and life exemplified a profound understanding of the Gospel as a message meant for all people, regardless of background or cultural identity. This inclusivity shaped his approach to evangelism, community-building, and doctrine, laying the groundwork for a Church that would transcend divisions and welcome diversity. Barnabas's inclusive and ecumenical vision reflects a commitment to the unity and universality of the Christian faith, an understanding that the love of Christ was intended to reach every corner of the world and to bring people together as one.

The foundation of Barnabas's inclusive vision can be traced to his early experiences with the Church in Jerusalem and his work in Antioch. Jerusalem was the birthplace of the Christian movement, rooted in Jewish tradition and customs, but as the message of Jesus spread beyond Judea, it encountered new cultures, languages, and beliefs. Barnabas, a Hellenistic Jew from Cyprus, was uniquely positioned to understand both the traditional Jewish context and the more cosmopolitan, diverse communities that would become the heart of the Christian movement. His openness to these different perspectives enabled him to see the potential for a truly universal Church, one that would not require cultural conformity but would honor each believer's unique identity within the body of Christ.

Barnabas's inclusive approach became especially evident in Antioch, one of the first cities where the Gospel was embraced by Gentiles in significant numbers. When Barnabas arrived in Antioch, he recognized the grace of God at work among these new believers, who came from various backgrounds and did not adhere to traditional Jewish customs. Rather than imposing Jewish practices on them, Barnabas encouraged their faith and welcomed them into the Christian community. His response to the Gentile believers at Antioch set a precedent for inclusivity, showing that the Church was not a place for rigid boundaries but a space where all who professed faith in Christ could find a home. This spirit of inclusion would become a defining characteristic of the early Church, one that allowed it to grow and thrive across diverse cultures.

Barnabas's inclusive vision extended beyond mere acceptance; he actively advocated for the rights and dignity of Gentile believers. His role at the Council of Jerusalem highlights his commitment to an inclusive Church. Faced with a divisive question—whether Gentile converts should be required to follow Jewish laws and customs—Barnabas stood alongside Paul to argue that faith in Christ was sufficient for salvation. This stance was radical, challenging long-standing religious traditions and expectations. For Barnabas, the central truth of the Gospel was that Christ's love was freely given to all, and that the barriers of ethnicity, culture, and tradition could no longer define one's relationship with God. By advocating for Gentile inclusion, Barnabas helped shape a Church that would embrace all people, a Church that reflected the global and timeless nature of the Christian message.

His inclusive vision was also marked by a sensitivity to the cultural contexts of those he evangelized. Barnabas understood that faith could take root in various cultures without requiring the erasure of local customs or identities. He did not seek to impose a single cultural model of Christianity but instead fostered a faith that could be expressed in diverse ways. This sensitivity allowed him to connect with people from different backgrounds, meeting them where they were and helping them understand the Gospel within their own cultural frameworks. Barnabas's approach reflects an ecumenical spirit that respected differences and sought unity without uniformity—a vision that allowed the Church to grow organically across different societies.

Another key aspect of Barnabas's inclusive vision was his belief in the transformative power of grace and forgiveness. His decision to mentor John Mark, even after the young man had abandoned a previous mission, reveals Barnabas's commitment to seeing potential and goodness in others, regardless of their past. This willingness to offer second chances reflects a theology rooted in redemption and renewal, a belief that each person has the capacity to grow and contribute to the Christian community. By extending grace to John Mark, Barnabas embodied the inclusivity he preached, showing that the Church was a place for those who were willing to learn, change, and serve. His actions underscored a vision of the Church as a community that embraces imperfection, fosters growth, and sees every believer as a valuable member of the body of Christ.

Barnabas's inclusive and ecumenical vision also included a strong emphasis on unity. In his role as a mediator and peacemaker, he worked to bring together believers from different backgrounds, ensuring that cultural and doctrinal differences did not fracture the community. His efforts at the Council of Jerusalem and his advocacy for Gentile believers illustrate his dedication to maintaining harmony within the Church. Barnabas understood that unity was essential for the strength and survival of the Christian faith, and he worked tirelessly to foster a spirit of cooperation and mutual respect. His approach set a standard for how the Church could navigate its differences, teaching believers to prioritize shared faith and love over minor disagreements.

The ecumenical aspect of Barnabas's vision is further evidenced in his approach to scripture and doctrine. He encouraged a way of interpreting scripture that allowed for multiple perspectives, a practice that would prove essential as the Church encountered new cultures and philosophies. Barnabas's

Christ-centered approach to scripture allowed believers to see the Old Testament in a new light, understanding its teachings as pointing toward Christ and the new covenant. This interpretative flexibility enabled the early Church to connect with diverse communities, creating a theology that was both grounded in tradition and open to new insights. Barnabas's ecumenical approach to doctrine encouraged a faith that was intellectually rich, spiritually profound, and adaptable to different cultural contexts.

Barnabas's life and ministry illustrate an understanding that the Church is not an exclusive club but a community that reflects the breadth and depth of God's love for humanity. His vision invites believers to embrace a faith that is welcoming, compassionate, and inclusive, a faith that seeks to break down barriers rather than build them. Barnabas's example challenges the Church to continually expand its understanding of inclusivity, to see diversity as a strength rather than a threat, and to welcome all who seek Christ with open arms.

The legacy of Barnabas's inclusive and ecumenical vision continues to resonate in the modern Church, reminding believers that the Gospel is meant for all people, regardless of nationality, culture, or social status. His example calls Christians to embrace a global perspective, to see themselves as part of a universal body that spans every corner of the earth. In a world where divisions often seem insurmountable, Barnabas's vision offers a model for unity, teaching that the Church's strength lies in its ability to bring together people of all backgrounds in a common faith.

In addition to shaping early Christian communities, Barnabas's inclusivity and ecumenism have inspired ecumenical movements throughout Church history, fostering dialogue and cooperation among different Christian traditions. His approach encourages Christians to seek common ground, to focus on shared beliefs, and to work together to advance the message of Christ. Barnabas's vision invites the Church to see itself not as a collection of isolated groups but as a single family, united by a shared mission and a common love for God.

In reflecting on Barnabas's life, believers are reminded of the importance of creating a Church that reflects the inclusive love of Christ. His example challenges Christians to reach beyond their comfort zones, to welcome those who are different, and to build bridges of understanding and respect. Barnabas's legacy as a champion of inclusivity and ecumenism invites the Church to continue his work, to strive for a unity that honors diversity, and to pursue a mission that welcomes all people into the fold of God's love.

Through his inclusive and ecumenical vision, Barnabas left a legacy that continues to inspire the Church to be a place of welcome, compassion, and unity. His life serves as a testament to the power of the Gospel to transcend human boundaries and to bring people together in a common faith. Barnabas's example calls the Church to live out its calling as a beacon of hope, a place where all are valued, and a community that reflects the boundless love of Christ. His legacy reminds believers that the true strength of the Church lies not in uniformity but in its ability to embrace and celebrate the diverse tapestry of God's people, united in faith, hope, and love.

Chapter 25
Relics and Traditions

As the legacy of Barnabas grew within the Christian community, so did the reverence for the physical remnants and symbols associated with his life and ministry. The importance of relics and traditions surrounding Barnabas not only provided a tangible connection to this revered apostle but also reinforced the early Church's sense of continuity and unity with its founding figures. From sacred objects believed to be linked to Barnabas to stories passed down across generations, these relics and traditions became important components of Christian devotion, serving as symbols of faith and reminders of the virtues that Barnabas embodied.

The earliest and most significant relic associated with Barnabas is believed to be his tomb, which, according to tradition, is located in Cyprus, near the city of Salamis where he is thought to have been martyred. The story of Barnabas's burial and the preservation of his tomb emerged as part of the Christian narrative in Cyprus, a place where his impact had been profound. According to local tradition, Barnabas's remains were discovered centuries after his death, still holding a copy of the Gospel of Matthew on his chest. This discovery reinforced the belief that Barnabas was a guardian of the faith, a protector of the Gospel who continued to serve the Church even after his death. This relic of the Gospel of Matthew became an object of reverence, symbolizing Barnabas's unwavering commitment to Christ's teachings and his role in spreading the Good News.

The tomb of Barnabas became a site of pilgrimage for early Christians, especially for those in Cyprus and the surrounding regions. Believers traveled to his resting place to seek inspiration, healing, and a sense of connection to the early days of the Church. For many, visiting the tomb of Barnabas was a way to honor his legacy and to express gratitude for his work in spreading the Gospel. Pilgrimages to his tomb provided an opportunity for believers to reflect on his virtues—his courage, humility, and inclusivity—and to seek his intercession. These pilgrimages not only reinforced devotion to Barnabas but also strengthened the bonds within the Christian community, bringing believers together in shared acts of remembrance and reverence.

Throughout the centuries, churches and monasteries dedicated to Barnabas were established in Cyprus and beyond, serving as places of worship, study, and reflection. These sacred spaces often featured artwork, icons, and stained glass depicting scenes from Barnabas's life—his missionary journeys, his acts of compassion, and his martyrdom. These depictions allowed believers to visualize and connect with Barnabas, providing a sense of immediacy and closeness to this early apostle. The dedication of churches and shrines in his honor underscored the respect and veneration that Barnabas commanded within the Christian community, serving as a testament to his enduring influence and as places where his teachings could continue to inspire new generations of believers.

In addition to physical relics, traditions associated with Barnabas's life and work began to take root, particularly among the Christian communities in Cyprus. Stories and customs that celebrated his life became woven into the fabric of Cypriot Christianity, and annual feast days commemorated his contributions to the Church. In the Eastern Orthodox Church, for example, the feast of St. Barnabas is celebrated on June 11, a date that serves as a time for reflection on his life and for honoring his role in spreading the Gospel. On this day, believers gather for special liturgies, prayers, and readings from scripture that highlight Barnabas's dedication to Christ. Through these liturgical practices, Barnabas's memory is kept alive, his life becoming a touchstone for the faith and devotion of countless Christians.

Many of the traditions surrounding Barnabas are rooted in the values and virtues he embodied. Stories of his compassion, his courage in the face of adversity, and his dedication to unity became central themes in Christian teaching and storytelling. These traditions painted Barnabas as a model for believers, encouraging them to live lives marked by faith, humility, and service. In particular, his willingness to accept and include Gentiles into the Christian community became a symbol of the Church's mission to reach all people, a tradition that emphasized the universality of Christ's message. Through these stories, Barnabas became more than a historical figure; he became a symbol of the inclusive and compassionate spirit of the Gospel.

As the Church spread throughout Europe and the Middle East, devotion to Barnabas also grew. His reputation as a man of deep faith and boundless encouragement made him a popular figure, especially among communities seeking to navigate divisions and build unity. His image often appeared in artwork and illuminated manuscripts, reminding believers of his role as a unifier and protector of the early Church. These artistic depictions were not merely decorative; they served as visual representations of the virtues Barnabas embodied, reminding believers of his example. In monasteries, his story was taught as a part of monastic formation, with his life serving as a guide for those pursuing lives of faith, service, and contemplation.

Barnabas's role as a peacemaker also became a key part of his legacy, particularly in areas where Christian communities faced internal strife. The tradition of invoking Barnabas's intercession in times of discord reflects a belief that he could offer guidance and wisdom to bring about reconciliation. His reputation for building bridges between different factions and promoting unity made him an ideal intercessor for communities seeking peace and harmony. This tradition of calling upon Barnabas's intercession extended beyond his lifetime, as believers continued to see him as a mediator and a source of strength in times of conflict.

Over time, the relics and traditions associated with Barnabas became an integral part of Christian spirituality, providing believers with a means of connecting with the early Church and with the values that Barnabas exemplified. His legacy as a source of encouragement, as a man who welcomed all into the fold, and as a defender of the faith was preserved through these customs, allowing each generation to find inspiration in his story. Relics, icons, and feast days offered a tangible connection to Barnabas, while the stories of his life continued to serve as moral and spiritual lessons for believers seeking to live lives of faith and devotion.

In the modern Church, the traditions surrounding Barnabas remind Christians of the importance of honoring those who came before, of recognizing the sacrifices and contributions that laid the foundation for the faith. His life calls believers to consider the impact of their own actions, to see themselves as part of a legacy that spans centuries, and to honor that legacy through lives of service, compassion, and unity. Barnabas's example continues to encourage Christians to live out their faith with integrity, to embrace the spirit of inclusivity he championed, and to carry forward the Gospel with the same passion and dedication that he demonstrated.

Through the relics and traditions associated with Barnabas, the Church is invited to reflect on the enduring power of faith to shape lives and communities. His memory serves as a reminder of the values that define the Christian life, values that transcend time and place, inspiring believers across generations. The legacy of Barnabas as preserved in relics, artwork, and customs offers a living connection to the past, a source of strength and encouragement for the present, and a beacon of hope for the future. His story, celebrated and remembered through these traditions, invites each believer to join in the ongoing mission of the Church, to be a force for love, unity, and transformation in the world.

In honoring the relics and traditions of Barnabas, Christians are reminded that faith is a journey, one shaped by those who have gone before and sustained by the practices that connect us to the past. His life serves as an example of the ways in which devotion, humility, and a commitment to the Gospel can leave a lasting mark on the world. Through his relics and the traditions that celebrate his memory, Barnabas continues to inspire believers to pursue lives of faith, to build communities of love, and to follow the path he helped to illuminate—a path that leads ever closer to Christ.

Chapter 26
Cultural Influence

Barnabas, though primarily known as a central figure in the early Church, also had a significant cultural influence that extended beyond his role as an apostle. His life and legacy left an indelible mark on the societies he encountered, shaping not only the religious practices of the time but also the cultural, social, and intellectual landscapes of the Mediterranean world. Barnabas's influence is visible in the arts, in literature, and in the values that underpinned the Christian communities he helped to establish. His approach to inclusivity, his passion for unity, and his emphasis on compassion resonated not only within the Church but also in the broader culture, where his example continued to inspire and guide individuals and communities through the centuries.

The social and cultural landscape of Barnabas's time was one of diversity and complexity. The Roman Empire spanned multiple continents, incorporating a wide range of beliefs, practices, and customs. As an apostle with Hellenistic roots, Barnabas was well-suited to navigate this multicultural world. His experiences in Cyprus, Antioch, and various regions in Asia Minor exposed him to a variety of cultures and perspectives, which informed his approach to evangelism and community-building. Barnabas's ability to connect with diverse groups and to communicate the Gospel in a way that respected local traditions allowed Christianity to grow organically, adapting to new cultural contexts while retaining its core message. This adaptability became a defining feature of the early Church, one that would enable it to flourish across different societies and eventually reshape the cultural identity of the Mediterranean world.

In his missionary work, Barnabas promoted a vision of Christianity that was inclusive and transcultural, a vision that resonated deeply with communities from different backgrounds. His welcoming approach to Gentiles in Antioch, for instance, demonstrated a radical openness that challenged cultural norms and traditional boundaries. By advocating for the full inclusion of Gentiles without requiring adherence to Jewish customs, Barnabas helped establish a Christianity that could be embraced by people from all walks of life. This inclusivity not only expanded the reach of the Church but also influenced the broader cultural understanding of community, challenging prevailing notions of identity and belonging. Barnabas's actions encouraged people to see themselves as part of a larger spiritual family, fostering a sense of unity that transcended ethnic and cultural divides.

Barnabas's emphasis on compassion and charity also had a profound cultural impact, shaping the social values of the communities he touched. His acts of generosity—such as selling his land to support the early Christian community—set a precedent for charitable giving that became a hallmark of Christian ethics. This spirit of generosity inspired early Christian communities to prioritize the well-being of all members, creating a culture of mutual support and care. Barnabas's example encouraged believers to view wealth as a means of serving others, rather than as a personal possession, a revolutionary idea in a society where wealth and status were often closely linked. This shift in values helped to establish the Church as a place of refuge and support, a community that prioritized compassion and care for the vulnerable, and these values gradually permeated the broader society, influencing social norms and expectations.

In addition to his influence on social values, Barnabas's life and teachings also left a lasting mark on the arts. His legacy inspired a rich tradition of storytelling, iconography, and literature that celebrated his virtues and commemorated his contributions to the faith. In early Christian art, Barnabas is often depicted as a wise and compassionate figure, a portrayal that reflects his role as an encourager and unifier. These images served as visual representations of the values he embodied, offering believers a model of faithfulness, humility, and courage. The portrayal of Barnabas in Christian art also reinforced his status as a beloved figure, a symbol of the early Church's commitment to inclusivity and service.

Barnabas's influence extended into Christian literature as well, where his life and ministry were celebrated in hymns, stories, and historical accounts. The *Acts of Barnabas*, an apocryphal text attributed to John Mark, recounts the apostle's missionary journeys and martyrdom, highlighting his dedication to the Gospel and his unwavering faith. Although not considered canonical, this text and others like it contributed to the development of a Christian literary tradition that honored the lives of the apostles and preserved their teachings. Through these writings, Barnabas's story continued to inspire generations of believers, providing a spiritual and moral example that resonated across cultural boundaries. These accounts, whether factual or embellished by legend, helped to establish Barnabas as a figure of enduring cultural significance, a man whose life transcended the limitations of time and place.

Barnabas's approach to leadership and community-building also influenced the development of Christian institutions, particularly in regions where he had a direct impact, such as Cyprus and Antioch. His emphasis on collaboration, mentorship, and mutual support informed the organizational structure of the early Church, shaping its practices and priorities. The establishment of councils, communal worship practices, and systems of support for widows, orphans, and the poor can be traced back to the values that Barnabas and other apostles instilled in the fledgling Christian communities. This organizational structure, grounded in principles of equality and compassion, became a defining feature of the Christian community and influenced the way the Church interacted with the broader society. Over time, these practices contributed to the development of a social and ethical framework that shaped not only Christian institutions but also the societies in which they were embedded.

Barnabas's cultural influence is perhaps most evident in the legacy of inclusivity he championed. His efforts to welcome Gentiles and his dedication to unity left a profound mark on the Church's identity, shaping it as a faith that was open to all. This inclusivity challenged the divisions of his time, offering a model of community that transcended ethnic, social, and economic boundaries. Barnabas's vision of a united Church inspired later Christian thinkers and leaders, reinforcing the belief that the Gospel was meant to reach all people and that the Church was called to embody this universality. His legacy laid the groundwork for ecumenical efforts within Christianity, encouraging believers to seek common ground and to work together despite their differences. This commitment to inclusivity has remained a core value within the Church, a reflection of Barnabas's influence and his belief in a faith that welcomes all.

In the centuries following Barnabas's death, his influence continued to be felt as the Church expanded into new regions and encountered new cultures. His example of adapting the Gospel to different cultural contexts without compromising its core message served as a model for missionaries and Church leaders. Barnabas's approach provided a framework for evangelism that respected local customs and encouraged cultural expression within the framework of Christian belief. This adaptability contributed to the spread of Christianity across diverse societies, enabling it to become a truly global faith. Through his legacy, Barnabas demonstrated that the Gospel could flourish in any cultural context, that it was not bound by geography or ethnicity but was a message of hope and redemption for all.

Today, Barnabas's cultural influence remains relevant as the Church continues to navigate questions of identity, diversity, and unity. His life and legacy challenge modern Christians to embrace a faith that is both inclusive and adaptable, a faith that can respond to the needs and values of contemporary society while remaining true to its foundational teachings. Barnabas's example invites believers to engage with the world around them, to find ways of expressing the Gospel that resonate with people from all backgrounds, and to create communities that reflect the universal love of Christ.

Barnabas's cultural influence is a testament to the transformative power of a life lived in service to God and to others. His legacy reminds Christians that faith is not only about personal belief but about creating a positive impact on the world, about shaping communities and societies in ways that reflect the values of the Kingdom of God. Through his actions, Barnabas showed that the Gospel could touch every aspect of life, that it had the power to inspire compassion, to foster unity, and to elevate culture. His life serves as a reminder that the Church is called not only to preserve its teachings but to share them in ways that speak to each generation, to embody a faith that is as relevant today as it was in the time of the apostles.

In honoring Barnabas's cultural legacy, the Church is reminded of its role as a force for good in the world, a community that is called to reflect the love, inclusivity, and compassion that Barnabas so fully embodied. His life and influence continue to inspire believers to engage with their cultures, to be agents of positive change, and to carry forward a faith that transcends boundaries, a faith that remains rooted in the teachings of Christ and open to the world. Through his legacy, Barnabas calls Christians to build a Church that is both deeply rooted and universally welcoming, a Church that speaks to the hearts of people across all cultures and times.

Chapter 27
Patron of Artists

In the centuries following his life, Barnabas came to be recognized not only as a missionary and spiritual leader but also as an inspiring figure for artists. His example of humility, courage, and encouragement resonated deeply with the creative community, and he became a patron of those who sought to express faith through art. Through their work, artists found a way to honor Barnabas's legacy, translating his virtues and life story into paintings, sculptures, stained glass, and other forms of artistic expression. As the patron of artists, Barnabas continues to influence and inspire those who seek to bring beauty, meaning, and faith into the world through their craft.

Barnabas's journey, marked by resilience, faith, and inclusivity, offered artists rich themes to explore. His life embodied qualities that resonate with the creative spirit—a deep compassion for others, an ability to see potential in unlikely places, and an openness to diverse perspectives. For artists, Barnabas symbolized the ideal of using one's talents in service to something greater, reminding them that creativity is a divine gift meant to inspire, uplift, and bring people closer to God. By invoking Barnabas as their patron, artists embraced his spirit of encouragement, finding in his life a model for using their skills to build a more compassionate and spiritually aware world.

In the Middle Ages, Barnabas began to appear frequently in religious art, often portrayed in scenes from his missionary journeys or depicted alongside Paul in their shared work. In these images, Barnabas is usually shown as a compassionate figure, with open hands and a gentle expression, symbolizing his welcoming spirit and his dedication to spreading the Gospel. These portrayals served as visual reminders of his character, inspiring viewers to consider the virtues of kindness, humility, and courage that he exemplified. For artists, capturing Barnabas's likeness was a way of honoring his memory while also meditating on the values he stood for, allowing his image to serve as a source of inspiration for generations.

Artists also found in Barnabas's life a symbol of resilience and perseverance—qualities essential to the creative process. Just as Barnabas faced opposition and setbacks in his ministry, artists often confront obstacles in their work, from personal doubts to external criticism. By looking to Barnabas as a patron, artists drew strength from his example, finding encouragement to persist in their creative pursuits despite the challenges. His life demonstrated that faith and dedication could carry one through adversity, a message that resonated deeply within the artistic community. This connection to Barnabas helped to forge a bond between the spiritual and creative aspects of the artistic vocation, reinforcing the idea that art is a form of devotion that can serve as a powerful vehicle for expressing faith and truth.

Barnabas's influence extended to the architecture of churches and monasteries dedicated to his memory, where artists created magnificent spaces designed to inspire awe and reflection. These sacred spaces often featured frescoes, stained glass, and carvings depicting scenes from his life, allowing worshippers to experience the story of Barnabas through visual storytelling. The architecture and artwork in these buildings were not simply decorative; they served a didactic purpose, teaching believers about Barnabas's virtues and reminding them of his legacy as they entered into prayer. This integration of art and faith transformed these spaces into places where the spirit of Barnabas lived on, inviting each visitor to reflect on his life and to seek a deeper connection with God.

During the Renaissance, artists continued to honor Barnabas, often exploring his role as a teacher and mentor. In paintings and sculptures, Barnabas was depicted guiding Paul, preaching in synagogues, or welcoming new believers. These works emphasized his role as an encourager, a man who saw potential in others and who was willing to help them grow in their faith. Renaissance artists were inspired by Barnabas's dedication to unity and his openness to diverse perspectives, qualities that aligned with the Renaissance spirit of exploration and curiosity. By portraying Barnabas, artists of this period celebrated a figure who embodied the ideal of using one's gifts for the greater good, a theme that resonated within the humanist ideals of the era.

One of the most notable aspects of Barnabas's influence on art is his role as a symbol of reconciliation and unity, themes that are deeply woven into the Christian artistic tradition. In icons, mosaics, and paintings, Barnabas is often depicted as a bridge between people—whether between Jews and Gentiles, or between different factions within the Church. Artists embraced this aspect of his life, using their work to convey messages of harmony, forgiveness, and understanding. Barnabas's legacy inspired artists to create pieces that encouraged viewers to look beyond divisions and to seek common ground, fostering a spirit of peace and unity through their art. His image became a visual reminder of the call to embrace others with compassion and to work toward reconciliation, ideals that remain relevant across generations and cultures.

Barnabas's legacy as a patron of artists is not only about the subjects of the art but also about the creative process itself. His life exemplified the idea of being open to inspiration, of listening to the guidance of the Holy Spirit, and of sharing one's gifts with others. These qualities resonate deeply within the artistic vocation, where creativity is often seen as a divine spark, an inspiration that moves through the artist to bring something beautiful and meaningful into the world. By looking to Barnabas as a guide, artists are reminded that their work has the potential to touch lives, to bring people closer to the divine, and to inspire a deeper sense of connection with God and each other.

In the modern era, Barnabas continues to inspire artists who seek to create works that are not only aesthetically pleasing but spiritually significant. His example encourages contemporary artists to engage with themes of faith, compassion, and unity, to use their talents in ways that contribute to a more loving and understanding world. The values he embodied—openness, encouragement, and perseverance—remain relevant for artists today, who often find themselves navigating a complex cultural landscape in which art can serve as a bridge between faith and the broader world. Barnabas's legacy reminds them that art has the power to convey profound truths, to reach across divides, and to touch the hearts of those who encounter it.

Barnabas's influence also extends to the concept of art as a form of ministry. His life demonstrates that creativity can be a form of worship, a way of honoring God by expressing the beauty and complexity of the divine through visual and tactile forms. By viewing their work as a continuation of Barnabas's mission to encourage, uplift, and inspire, artists can find a sense of purpose and fulfillment in their craft. His legacy invites them to see their art as a way of contributing to the Church's mission, of using their gifts to illuminate the teachings of Christ and to bring joy, peace, and reflection to others.

The continued devotion to Barnabas as a patron of artists serves as a testament to his lasting impact on the Church and on the creative community. His life and legacy challenge artists to use their talents with intention, to seek beauty in the world around them, and to create works that reflect the love and truth of the Gospel. Barnabas's example encourages them to embrace the creative process with humility and reverence, to see their art as a means of connecting with others and with God, and to approach their work with the same spirit of encouragement that defined his life.

In honoring Barnabas as their patron, artists are reminded that their craft is more than a profession; it is a calling, a vocation that has the power to inspire, heal, and transform. His life serves as a guide for those who seek to use their gifts in service to others, offering a model of creativity rooted in faith, compassion, and a desire to bring light into the world. Through his legacy, Barnabas continues to be a source of encouragement for artists everywhere, inviting them to carry forward his spirit of kindness, courage, and unity in their own work.

As the patron of artists, Barnabas remains a beloved figure whose life and example resonate deeply within the creative community. His legacy challenges artists to look beyond themselves, to seek meaning and purpose in their work, and to create with a heart open to the divine. Through their art, they honor his memory, bringing to life the values he cherished and sharing his message of love, hope, and faith with the world. Barnabas's influence on art serves as a reminder that beauty and creativity are gifts from God, gifts that have the power to uplift the human spirit and to draw people closer to the eternal.

Chapter 28
Accounts of Miracles and Healings

Among the early followers of Christ, Barnabas was revered not only as a teacher and evangelist but also as a man through whom God worked wondrous acts. Accounts of miracles and healings attributed to Barnabas circulated within the early Christian community, serving as powerful testimonies of faith and divine intervention. These stories, whether legendary or rooted in historical events, reinforced the belief in God's active presence in the world and highlighted Barnabas as a vessel of divine power. Through these miracles and healings, Barnabas's legacy took on a supernatural dimension, embodying the transformative, life-giving force of the Gospel he preached.

One of the earliest accounts of Barnabas's miracles comes from his missionary journeys with Paul. In these early years of the Church, miracles were often seen as signs that authenticated the apostles' message, providing undeniable evidence of the power of Christ. As Barnabas traveled across cities and regions, many believed he possessed the spiritual gifts of healing and prophecy, and stories of miraculous events quickly spread among believers. These accounts often depict Barnabas laying hands on the sick, casting out evil spirits, and offering prayers that brought physical and spiritual relief. For the early Christian community, these acts were a visible expression of God's love and mercy, an affirmation that Christ's power continued to work through His followers.

One notable story takes place during Barnabas's time in Cyprus, where he is said to have performed several miraculous acts that deeply impacted the local population. According to tradition, Barnabas healed those suffering from physical ailments, restored sight to the blind, and even revived individuals who were believed to be close to death. These acts of healing were seen as signs of divine grace, manifestations of a faith that could transcend natural limitations. The people of Cyprus, already familiar with Barnabas's role as a local leader, came to regard him as a holy man through whom God's presence was made real. His reputation as a healer helped to spread the Christian message, drawing crowds who were both curious and hopeful for miracles of their own.

One particular miracle attributed to Barnabas is said to have occurred in the presence of local officials, where he healed a man who had been paralyzed. This act, witnessed by prominent figures in the community, carried significant weight and lent authority to Barnabas's mission. Such public miracles not only demonstrated the power of Christ but also disrupted the social and religious norms of the time, as local leaders and religious figures saw their influence challenged by the growing number of believers inspired by Barnabas's deeds. These miraculous acts served as both spiritual signs and practical demonstrations of God's power, compelling people from various walks of life to question their beliefs and to consider the teachings of Christ.

Miraculous healings attributed to Barnabas were not limited to physical ailments; many stories tell of emotional and spiritual healing as well. Barnabas's compassion and gentleness, coupled with his deep faith, are said to have brought peace to those suffering from inner torment, doubt, or grief. His words and prayers were known to soothe troubled minds, to bring comfort to the grieving, and to inspire hope in those who had lost their way. For many, Barnabas was not just a healer of bodies but a healer of souls, a man whose presence brought a sense of divine peace. These accounts highlight Barnabas's role as a shepherd of the Christian flock, a guide who cared for the whole person, both body and spirit.

Stories of exorcisms attributed to Barnabas also circulated within early Christian communities. In these accounts, he is said to have confronted and cast out unclean spirits, bringing freedom and relief to those who were afflicted. These acts of deliverance were regarded as signs of the authority Christ had entrusted to His apostles, a reminder that God's kingdom had the power to overcome the forces of darkness. Barnabas's role in these exorcisms reinforced the belief that spiritual forces were actively at work in the world, both good and evil, and that the Christian mission included a commitment to healing and liberation. These exorcisms served as dramatic testimonies of God's power and love, emphasizing the Church's role in bringing light into dark places.

Another dimension of Barnabas's miraculous influence lies in stories of prophetic visions and words of knowledge. According to tradition, Barnabas possessed the gift of insight, a spiritual sensitivity that allowed him to perceive truths that were hidden to others. These prophetic gifts were often seen as confirmations of his deep connection with the Holy Spirit, as well as evidence of his devotion and faith. Stories tell of Barnabas offering words of encouragement that foretold future blessings or offering wisdom that guided others in moments of crisis. His ability to discern spiritual truths and to speak with divine authority marked him as a prophetic figure, a man through whom God communicated His will to the early Church. These gifts further solidified Barnabas's reputation as a holy man, a figure who embodied the spiritual and mystical dimensions of the Christian faith.

The miraculous accounts surrounding Barnabas were not only personal affirmations of faith for individuals but also served a communal purpose, strengthening the resolve of the early Church. In a time of persecution and opposition, these stories of miracles and healings offered hope and reassurance. They reminded believers that God was with them, actively working in their midst through figures like Barnabas. His life became a symbol of divine protection and presence, a reminder that God's grace could overcome any obstacle. For a fledgling community facing hostility, these stories of Barnabas's miracles provided both spiritual sustenance and a rallying point for collective faith.

Over the centuries, stories of Barnabas's miraculous acts have continued to inspire and resonate within the Christian tradition. Pilgrims who visited his tomb and holy sites dedicated to his memory often sought healing, believing that his intercession could bring them relief from suffering. These pilgrimages became acts of faith in themselves, expressions of trust in the power of God that had once worked through Barnabas and that believers hoped would touch them as well. The veneration of Barnabas as a healer and miracle worker continued, with many Christians invoking his name in prayer for healing and comfort. His legacy as a man through whom miracles were performed continues to hold significance for those who seek divine intervention in their own lives.

In the modern Church, the accounts of Barnabas's miracles invite believers to reflect on the nature of faith and the power of God to work beyond human limitations. His life serves as a reminder that miracles are not confined to the past but are expressions of a God who is eternally present and active. Barnabas's example challenges Christians to be open to the possibility of the miraculous, to approach their faith with a sense of wonder, and to trust that God's power can bring transformation in ways that may defy human understanding. His story invites believers to see the world with eyes of faith, to recognize the potential for God's grace to work in unexpected and extraordinary ways.

Barnabas's legacy as a worker of miracles and healer of hearts is a testament to the boundless compassion and mercy of God. His life exemplifies the Christian belief in a God who heals, restores, and brings new life to all who seek Him. Through the miracles attributed to Barnabas, believers are reminded of the hope and joy that come from faith, of the healing power that can flow from a life dedicated to God, and of the enduring presence of Christ's love in the world. His story continues to inspire

Christians to pray for healing, to trust in divine grace, and to seek the miraculous in their own journeys of faith.

In honoring Barnabas as a worker of miracles and a healer, the Church celebrates not only his life but the God who empowered him. His legacy serves as a bridge between the natural and the supernatural, a reminder that the Christian faith is a living faith, one in which God's presence is made manifest through acts of love, compassion, and grace. Through Barnabas's story, believers are invited to embrace a faith that is both humble and bold, a faith that acknowledges human frailty while trusting in divine strength. His legacy as a miracle worker endures as a testament to the transforming power of God and a beacon of hope for all who believe in the God who makes the impossible possible.

Chapter 29
Charisma and Spiritual Power

Barnabas, one of the most respected figures in the early Church, was known not only for his missionary work and deep compassion but also for his charisma and spiritual power. These qualities made him a magnetic figure whose influence extended far beyond words. His presence and spirit inspired courage, faith, and unity in others, qualities essential to building and sustaining the early Christian community. Barnabas's spiritual power was not about authority or domination but was rooted in humility, kindness, and a profound openness to the Holy Spirit. This charisma, combined with his faith and wisdom, made Barnabas a pivotal force in the spread of Christianity, leaving a legacy of spiritual strength that continues to inspire.

From his earliest days within the Christian community, Barnabas displayed a rare spiritual sensitivity and depth that set him apart. Described in Acts as "a good man, full of the Holy Spirit and of faith," Barnabas exuded a quality that drew people to him and made them feel seen, understood, and uplifted. His nickname—meaning "son of encouragement"—reflected his gift for nurturing faith in others, a charisma that went beyond mere friendliness to a genuine power of encouragement. This spiritual gift allowed him to bring out the best in others, whether in guiding a new believer, supporting Paul in his ministry, or mentoring John Mark despite his early setbacks. Barnabas's encouragement empowered others to embrace their own callings, magnifying the impact of his own work through the lives he inspired.

One of the defining aspects of Barnabas's charisma was his remarkable ability to unite people from different backgrounds, fostering a sense of community that transcended ethnic, social, and religious barriers. In Antioch, where Jewish and Gentile converts first mingled within a single community, Barnabas's presence was essential in promoting harmony and mutual respect. His spiritual power enabled him to act as a bridge between these diverse groups, helping them to see their shared faith as more important than any cultural or social distinctions. Barnabas's ability to foster unity was not only a testament to his character but also to his spiritual insight—a vision of the Church as a universal body bound together by love and faith. His charisma made him a natural leader, one who could bring people together and guide them toward a common purpose.

Another powerful manifestation of Barnabas's charisma was his courage. His faith imbued him with a fearlessness that allowed him to navigate dangerous situations and confront adversities with grace and resilience. Barnabas's courage was evident when he first embraced Paul, a former persecutor of Christians, and brought him into the fold. By welcoming Paul and introducing him to the apostles, Barnabas took a risk, trusting in Paul's transformation despite his past. This act of bravery reflected not only his faith in God's power to change lives but also his own spiritual strength and willingness to face potential backlash for his decisions. Barnabas's courage inspired others to approach their own challenges with trust and conviction, reinforcing the early Church's resolve in the face of opposition.

Barnabas's charisma also shone through in his profound humility. Unlike many charismatic leaders who seek attention or power, Barnabas consistently demonstrated a selflessness that further elevated his spiritual influence. He was content to let others take the spotlight, as seen in his relationship with Paul. Although Barnabas was initially the more prominent figure, he gracefully stepped back as Paul's influence grew, allowing Paul to assume a central role in the mission. This humility revealed a man who was deeply attuned to the mission's importance over personal recognition, showing that his spiritual power was grounded not in ego but in an authentic devotion to the Gospel. Barnabas's humility encouraged others to work together, fostering an environment where every contribution was valued and where the mission was placed above individual glory.

One of the most intriguing aspects of Barnabas's spiritual power was his openness to the guidance of the Holy Spirit. His ministry was characterized by a sensitivity to God's leading, a quality that allowed him to respond to challenges and opportunities with wisdom and discernment. Whether making decisions about where to preach, whom to support, or how to address conflicts within the community, Barnabas displayed a spiritual intuition that inspired confidence among his followers. His ability to listen deeply to the Spirit's promptings, coupled with his willingness to act upon them, made him a leader who was not only respected but trusted. This trust was a cornerstone of his charisma, a gift that encouraged others to place their faith in God's guidance.

Barnabas's spiritual power also manifested in his capacity for forgiveness and reconciliation. In a time when conflicts and misunderstandings could easily fracture the early Church, Barnabas was a stabilizing force who sought to mend divisions rather than exacerbate them. His decision to support John Mark, even after he had abandoned the mission once, reflects this capacity for forgiveness. By giving John Mark a second chance, Barnabas demonstrated the grace and patience that are hallmarks of true spiritual power. This example of reconciliation set a standard within the Church, encouraging others to practice forgiveness and to welcome those who had faltered back into the community. Barnabas's ability to foster reconciliation and healing further strengthened his influence, as believers saw in him a model of Christ's compassion and mercy.

The strength of Barnabas's spiritual power was also evident in his resilience. Despite facing persecution, hardship, and eventual martyrdom, Barnabas remained unwavering in his commitment to the mission. His resilience was not a stoic endurance but a joyful, hopeful strength that inspired those around him to persevere. This resilience was a gift of the Spirit, one that allowed Barnabas to confront suffering without losing his faith or his sense of purpose. His joy in the midst of trials served as a powerful testimony to the transformative power of the Gospel, a reminder to believers that true strength is found in surrender to God's will.

Through his charisma and spiritual power, Barnabas influenced the early Church in ways that transcended his direct actions. His example inspired a model of leadership that valued encouragement, humility, and a willingness to serve others selflessly. His life challenged believers to look beyond themselves, to see their own potential as vessels of God's grace, and to approach their faith with courage and compassion. Barnabas's spiritual power was not simply a gift for himself but a light that illuminated the path for others, a charisma that empowered them to pursue their own callings with confidence and dedication.

Today, Barnabas's legacy of spiritual power and charisma continues to inspire. His life reminds Christians of the importance of cultivating inner strength, humility, and openness to the Spirit, qualities that allow them to lead and serve in ways that honor God. Barnabas's example challenges believers to view charisma not as a means of personal influence but as a gift to be used for the common good, a way of bringing people closer to God and to one another. His spiritual power remains a source of encouragement for those who seek to live lives of integrity and faith, demonstrating that true charisma is rooted in a deep connection with the divine.

Barnabas's legacy encourages Christians to seek spiritual power that uplifts rather than dominates, that inspires rather than intimidates. His life shows that true power lies not in control or authority but in a gentle strength that draws others into a deeper relationship with God. Through his charisma, Barnabas embodied the heart of the Gospel, a message of love, unity, and hope that transcends time and place. His story invites each believer to reflect on their own sources of strength, to cultivate spiritual gifts that serve and inspire, and to become vessels of God's grace in the world.

In honoring Barnabas's spiritual power and charisma, the Church celebrates a life that exemplifies the very essence of Christian faith—a faith that transforms, uplifts, and empowers. His legacy is a call to all believers to live with courage, humility, and a heart open to the Spirit, to embrace the path of discipleship with a strength that is rooted not in human ambition but in divine love. Through Barnabas's example, Christians are reminded that charisma is a gift to be shared, a light that brightens the world and draws others closer to the beauty and truth of the Gospel.

Chapter 30
Intellectual Legacy

Barnabas's legacy is not only spiritual but intellectual; his contributions to the early Church extended beyond his work as an evangelist and leader to shaping the theological and intellectual foundations of Christianity. Known for his wisdom, insight, and deep understanding of both Jewish tradition and the teachings of Christ, Barnabas played an instrumental role in developing the intellectual framework that would sustain the early Church. His life and teachings encouraged believers to think deeply about the nature of faith, to explore the mysteries of God, and to engage in thoughtful discourse on the complexities of the Gospel message. Through his intellectual legacy, Barnabas left an indelible mark on Christian theology, inspiring generations of believers to pursue both knowledge and wisdom in their faith journeys.

Barnabas's intellectual influence began with his role as a bridge between Jewish and Gentile believers. As a Hellenistic Jew with strong ties to both Jewish culture and the wider Greco-Roman world, Barnabas possessed a unique perspective that allowed him to engage with diverse communities. He understood the deep theological roots of the Jewish faith while also appreciating the spiritual needs and philosophical perspectives of Gentile converts. His ability to contextualize the message of Christ in ways that resonated with different audiences helped create a foundation for a theology that was inclusive, adaptable, and intellectually robust. This approach set a precedent for Christian thought, emphasizing the importance of engaging with diverse perspectives and of crafting a theology that could speak to the hearts and minds of all people.

One of Barnabas's key intellectual contributions was his approach to interpreting scripture. Like many early Christians, Barnabas viewed the Old Testament as a sacred text that foreshadowed the coming of Christ. He believed that the events, prophecies, and symbols in the Hebrew scriptures found their fulfillment in Jesus, a perspective that became central to Christian theology. Barnabas's Christ-centered interpretation of scripture encouraged believers to see the Old Testament as part of a continuous story, one that led directly to the life, death, and resurrection of Christ. This interpretative approach provided a framework for understanding the relationship between the old and new covenants, offering a theological coherence that helped early Christians reconcile their Jewish heritage with their new faith in Christ.

The *Epistle of Barnabas*, traditionally attributed to him though its authorship remains uncertain, offers valuable insights into his theological views. This epistle exemplifies a method of interpretation known as typology, where Old Testament events, figures, and rituals are understood as symbols that prefigure New Testament realities. For example, the epistle reinterprets the concept of circumcision, suggesting that the true "circumcision" is not a physical act but the circumcision of the heart—a spiritual transformation that aligns one's life with God's will. This symbolic and allegorical approach to scripture reflected Barnabas's intellectual depth, offering early Christians a way to read the Bible that emphasized spiritual truths and encouraged a deeper exploration of God's mysteries. This typological interpretation would become a cornerstone of Christian thought, influencing generations of theologians and helping to shape the Church's understanding of scripture.

In addition to his contributions to biblical interpretation, Barnabas's emphasis on the centrality of faith over ritual marked an important shift in early Christian theology. While he respected Jewish customs and traditions, he believed that true righteousness came from faith in Christ rather than strict adherence to religious laws. This perspective was especially important in his dealings with Gentile converts, whom he welcomed without imposing the full weight of Jewish law upon them. Barnabas's teaching on faith over ritual underscored the transformative nature of the Gospel, emphasizing that salvation was a gift from God, not something that could be earned through human effort. This focus on faith as the foundation of the Christian life became a defining characteristic of Christian theology, encouraging believers to seek a personal relationship with God rather than relying on ritual observance alone.

Barnabas's intellectual legacy also included his advocacy for unity within the Church. His role in the Council of Jerusalem, where he argued for the inclusion of Gentile believers without requiring them to adhere to Jewish customs, demonstrated his commitment to a theology that valued inclusivity and harmony. Barnabas understood that theological divisions could threaten the unity of the Church, and he worked to ensure that doctrinal differences did not become sources of division. This emphasis on unity reflected his belief that the Church should be a reflection of the Kingdom of God—a diverse yet united body that transcended cultural and social boundaries. His vision of a unified Church continues to inspire ecumenical efforts within Christianity, encouraging believers to seek common ground and to work together in their pursuit of truth.

Barnabas's intellectual legacy extended beyond his own teachings; he also served as a mentor to other influential figures in the early Church, particularly Paul and John Mark. By guiding and supporting these figures, Barnabas helped to shape the intellectual trajectory of the Church, passing down his insights and perspectives to the next generation of leaders. His influence on Paul, in particular, was profound; their theological discussions and shared missionary experiences undoubtedly shaped Paul's thought and writings. The letters of Paul, which constitute a significant portion of the New Testament, reflect many themes that Barnabas championed—grace, unity, faith over ritual, and the inclusion of Gentiles in the Christian community. In this way, Barnabas's intellectual legacy lives on through the writings and teachings of those he mentored, a testament to his lasting impact on Christian thought.

Barnabas's intellectual approach to faith was not confined to theological concepts; he also emphasized the importance of moral and ethical conduct as expressions of one's beliefs. For Barnabas, intellectual understanding and moral action were inseparable—true knowledge of God led to a life of love, compassion, and service. This integration of faith and ethics was central to his teaching and set a standard for the Christian life, one that required believers not only to understand the Gospel but to live it out in their daily actions. Barnabas's emphasis on ethical conduct helped shape the moral teachings of the Church, encouraging believers to see their actions as reflections of their faith and as contributions to the witness of the Gospel in the world.

Another dimension of Barnabas's intellectual legacy is his role in shaping early Christian education. As Christianity spread and communities grew, the need for structured teaching and catechesis became increasingly important. Barnabas's commitment to teaching and mentoring helped establish a tradition of Christian education that emphasized both knowledge and spiritual growth. His example encouraged leaders to prioritize the intellectual formation of new believers, ensuring that they understood the foundations of their faith and could articulate it to others. This emphasis on education became a core value within the Church, leading to the development of catechetical schools, theological study, and the preservation of Christian writings. Barnabas's legacy as a teacher laid the groundwork for an intellectual tradition that valued inquiry, learning, and the pursuit of truth.

In modern times, Barnabas's intellectual legacy continues to inspire Christians to engage with their faith on a deeper level. His life challenges believers to explore the intellectual dimensions of their faith, to study scripture thoughtfully, and to seek understanding of God's mysteries. Barnabas's example encourages a faith that is both heartfelt and informed, a faith that embraces questions, seeks wisdom, and values the transformative power of knowledge. His legacy reminds Christians that intellectual exploration is not opposed to faith but is an essential part of a vibrant and mature relationship with God.

Barnabas's influence on Christian thought is a reminder that theology is not a static set of beliefs but a dynamic journey, one that requires openness, humility, and a willingness to grow. His life teaches that true understanding of God is rooted not only in doctrine but in love, compassion, and a desire to bring others into the light of the Gospel. Barnabas's intellectual legacy challenges believers to think deeply, to love fully, and to act justly, embodying a faith that is both intellectually rigorous and spiritually alive.

In honoring Barnabas's contributions to Christian thought, the Church celebrates a man who exemplified the harmony of intellect and faith, a teacher who invited others to explore the depths of God's love and wisdom. His life and teachings continue to inspire believers to pursue knowledge that leads to understanding, to engage with scripture in ways that reveal deeper truths, and to see theology as a living tradition that calls each generation to seek God with both heart and mind. Through his intellectual legacy, Barnabas invites Christians to a faith that is both thoughtful and transformative, a faith that shines as a light for all who seek truth.

Chapter 31
Artistic Representation

Across the centuries, Barnabas has been portrayed in sacred art that captures his image, spirit, and the values he represented. From illuminated manuscripts to stained glass windows, icons to sculptures, Barnabas's life has been rendered in forms meant not only to honor his legacy but to invite the faithful into contemplation of his role in the early Church. Artistic representations of Barnabas serve as visual theology, communicating to viewers the story of his life, his character, and his virtues, allowing the faithful to encounter his legacy in tangible ways that enrich spiritual reflection.

In early Christian iconography, Barnabas is often depicted alongside Paul, symbolizing their collaboration and mutual dedication to spreading the Gospel. These early images emphasize the unity and brotherhood that defined their partnership. Depictions show them either preaching together or in moments of shared prayer, highlighting the deep bond they shared and their joint commitment to the mission. These representations were especially meaningful for early Christians who valued the ideal of collaboration in faith and mission, encouraging believers to work together to further the message of Christ.

As Christianity developed, images of Barnabas began to focus on aspects of his character that set him apart as a unique figure within the faith. Paintings, murals, and mosaics began to depict Barnabas as a calm, contemplative figure, often with a scroll or book in his hand to signify his role as a teacher and writer. In these depictions, Barnabas appears approachable yet dignified, embodying the compassion and wisdom for which he was known. His gaze is often turned upward, symbolizing his connection to the divine, his devotion to God, and his openness to the Holy Spirit. These details reinforced his image as a man of deep faith, someone who devoted his life to understanding and spreading the teachings of Christ.

One of the central themes in artistic representations of Barnabas is his role as an encourager and peacemaker. Many icons depict him with outstretched hands or open arms, symbolizing his welcoming spirit and his willingness to embrace all who sought to follow Christ. This posture of openness mirrors his role in welcoming Gentile believers into the Church, making him a symbol of inclusivity and acceptance. Through these visual cues, artists conveyed Barnabas's spirit of hospitality and love, encouraging viewers to adopt the same openness and compassion in their own lives. The expression on Barnabas's face in such works often exudes warmth, suggesting his deep empathy and his ability to see the potential for faith in others.

Stained glass windows depicting Barnabas became common in medieval and Renaissance churches, particularly in Europe, where he was venerated for his role in the early Church. These stained glass works often show him in rich colors, set against scenes of his missionary work or moments of teaching. In one notable window from a Gothic cathedral, Barnabas is depicted healing the sick, reinforcing his reputation as a figure through whom God's healing grace flowed. The brilliant colors of these stained glass windows created a sense of awe and reverence, casting light and color into sacred spaces and allowing worshippers to feel his presence as they prayed and reflected on their faith.

During the Renaissance, representations of Barnabas took on new dimensions as artists explored human expressions of faith and divine encounters. Renaissance artists sought to capture the emotional depth of Barnabas's commitment, depicting him with expressions of contemplation and reverence. Paintings of Barnabas during this period often show him holding a cross or a

Bible, indicating his dedication to the Gospel and his role as a teacher. Some works also depict him in moments of prayer, his face illuminated with an inner light, symbolizing the guidance and inspiration of the Holy Spirit. These representations sought to convey not only his outer actions but also the inner life of devotion that defined him, inviting viewers to reflect on their own spiritual journeys.

In the Baroque period, artists focused on capturing dramatic scenes from Barnabas's life, portraying him in dynamic compositions that emphasized his missionary travels and moments of martyrdom. Baroque paintings often depict him in intense scenes, speaking to crowds or healing the sick, his figure animated with passion and movement. The use of shadow and light in these works created a sense of divine intervention, highlighting Barnabas as a man through whom God's presence was made manifest. In these dramatic depictions, Barnabas was presented as a powerful figure of action, a reminder to the faithful of the transformative power of faith and the call to serve with courage and conviction.

In Orthodox Christian iconography, Barnabas is often represented in a stylized, timeless manner, as is common with icons. In these depictions, he appears serene, with large, expressive eyes that gaze out to meet the viewer. Orthodox icons emphasize Barnabas's role as an apostle and martyr, using visual elements that communicate his sanctity and his close relationship with Christ. His garments are often richly colored and adorned with subtle symbols, reflecting his status as a holy figure. Icons of Barnabas invite the faithful to contemplate his life and to seek his intercession, serving as windows into the spiritual realm and as reminders of his ongoing presence within the communion of saints.

In addition to traditional paintings and icons, sculptures of Barnabas appear in cathedrals and religious spaces, often as part of larger scenes or tableaux depicting the apostles. Statues of Barnabas are typically shown with symbols that identify him, such as a cross or a book, indicating his role in spreading the

Gospel and his dedication to Christ. In some statues, Barnabas is depicted with a gentle smile, capturing the warmth and encouragement that he brought to those around him. Sculptures of Barnabas serve as physical reminders of his legacy, inviting the faithful to engage with his memory through a tactile, embodied form of devotion.

In modern times, artists have continued to explore Barnabas's legacy, creating works that reflect contemporary understandings of his life and virtues. Contemporary paintings, drawings, and installations often focus on themes of reconciliation, encouragement, and inclusivity, reflecting the values that Barnabas championed. In one notable modern painting, Barnabas is depicted standing between two groups, his hands raised in a gesture of peace, symbolizing his role as a unifier within the Church. Such works resonate with modern viewers who see Barnabas as a symbol of hope and a model for creating harmony within diverse communities.

Artistic representations of Barnabas across history highlight not only the enduring respect for his contributions to the Church but also the ways in which his life speaks to universal themes of compassion, humility, and faith. Through the evolving styles and interpretations of his image, Barnabas's legacy has been kept alive, allowing each generation to encounter him anew and to find inspiration in his example. Whether in the intricate lines of a medieval manuscript, the vibrant colors of a stained glass window, or the contemplative gaze of an Orthodox icon, Barnabas's image has become a touchstone of Christian art, a source of devotion and reflection that continues to uplift and inspire.

These visual depictions of Barnabas serve as more than mere art; they are acts of devotion, created by artists who sought to capture his spirit and to bring his story into the lives of the faithful. Each brushstroke, carving, and pane of glass reflects a deep reverence for Barnabas's life and a desire to share his story with the world. Through these representations, Barnabas's influence extends beyond words, reaching into the hearts of those who view these works and inviting them to engage with his legacy on a personal level.

In reflecting on the artistic legacy of Barnabas, believers are reminded of the power of art to communicate faith, to transcend words, and to evoke the divine. His life, depicted in countless forms across cultures and ages, serves as a testament to the enduring impact of a life devoted to God. The artistic representations of Barnabas call each viewer to consider the values he embodied, to see his example as a path toward deeper faith, and to find in his image a source of encouragement and hope. Through art, Barnabas's story lives on, a visual legacy that continues to inspire the faithful to follow in his footsteps and to seek a life of love, service, and devotion.

Chapter 32
Veneration and Popular Worship

As one of the early apostles who journeyed tirelessly to spread the message of Christianity, Barnabas's life has inspired profound veneration and devotion throughout Christian history. His legacy as a devoted servant of Christ, a compassionate guide, and a tireless advocate for unity made him a figure of deep reverence in the early Church, a devotion that has continued through centuries. This veneration has manifested in a variety of popular worship practices, feast days, pilgrimages, and prayers dedicated to Barnabas. His enduring presence within the devotional life of Christians around the world reflects a lasting admiration for his life and his unwavering commitment to the Gospel.

In the early centuries following Barnabas's martyrdom, stories of his life and his faith spread throughout the Mediterranean, particularly in Cyprus, where he was believed to have been buried. Christian communities, both in Cyprus and beyond, revered him as a local saint and a patron of unity and peace. His tomb in Cyprus became a pilgrimage destination for believers seeking to honor him and to pray for his intercession. Pilgrims journeyed from afar to pay homage at his resting place, often leaving offerings, flowers, or written prayers as signs of their devotion. The practice of pilgrimage to Barnabas's tomb symbolized the deep respect that believers held for him, and visiting his burial site became a way for the faithful to connect physically and spiritually with this early apostle and his mission.

The veneration of Barnabas also became formalized in the liturgical calendar, with feast days dedicated to his memory. In the Western Church, Barnabas's feast is celebrated on June 11, while Eastern Orthodox Christians honor him on this date as well, gathering for special services that commemorate his life, teachings, and sacrifices. These feast days are marked by readings from scripture, hymns that celebrate Barnabas's virtues, and prayers that ask for his intercession. The liturgical observance of his feast provides the faithful an opportunity to reflect on his legacy and to renew their own commitment to living lives of faith and service, inspired by Barnabas's example.

Throughout history, churches and monasteries dedicated to Barnabas have been established, further embedding his presence in the devotional practices of various Christian communities. These places of worship became spiritual centers where believers could gather to pray, reflect, and learn about Barnabas's life. Artwork and relics in these churches often depict scenes from Barnabas's missionary work, showing him preaching, healing, and leading others in faith. These churches became sanctuaries for believers seeking spiritual solace, where they could ask for Barnabas's intercession in their own struggles, trusting that he would offer his guidance and encouragement in their lives. The dedication of these sacred spaces in his honor also reinforced the Church's appreciation for Barnabas's contributions, embedding his memory in the physical and spiritual fabric of Christian communities.

One of the unique aspects of Barnabas's veneration is the way in which he is remembered not only as a saintly figure but as a relatable, compassionate friend to all who seek his guidance. Known as the "son of encouragement," Barnabas is frequently invoked by those who need strength and comfort, especially during times of hardship or doubt. Many Christians view him as a spiritual companion who understands their struggles and offers his support through prayer. In this way, Barnabas's veneration transcends the traditional boundaries of sainthood, allowing believers to feel a personal connection with him as a friend and mentor who walked a path similar to their own.

This personal connection is reflected in numerous prayers and devotions written in honor of Barnabas. Many of these prayers ask for his intercession to foster unity, peace, and courage. Devotees often turn to Barnabas in times of conflict, asking for his help in reconciling with others or finding harmony within their communities. In these prayers, Barnabas is invoked as a peacemaker and a healer, a man whose spirit continues to inspire believers to strive for unity and compassion. These prayers reflect the qualities that defined Barnabas's life—patience, kindness, and a commitment to bringing people together in faith.

Over time, certain customs and folk traditions developed around the veneration of Barnabas, especially in regions where his influence was particularly strong, such as Cyprus. Some believers wore medals or tokens bearing his image, believing these items would bring them protection, courage, and spiritual guidance. In some communities, blessings of fields, homes, or harvests were conducted on Barnabas's feast day, with the belief that his intercession would bring abundance and blessings. These folk traditions reveal the ways in which Barnabas became a part of the everyday lives of believers, his presence woven into the rhythms and rituals of daily life.

Another important dimension of Barnabas's veneration is his role as a patron for reconciliation and healing. Many Christians who seek healing for broken relationships, family conflicts, or community divisions turn to Barnabas, trusting in his ability to intercede for peace and restoration. Special devotions and novenas dedicated to Barnabas ask for his guidance in overcoming anger, prejudice, or misunderstanding. In these devotions, Barnabas is remembered as a champion of unity, a figure who worked tirelessly to bring people together in love and understanding. His legacy in promoting reconciliation continues to inspire Christians who wish to live in harmony with others, making him a beloved intercessor in times of relational strife.

In the Orthodox Christian tradition, Barnabas is also celebrated as a holy and wise teacher. Icons of Barnabas are often placed in homes, churches, and monasteries, where they serve as focal points for meditation and prayer. These icons depict Barnabas with expressions of serenity and wisdom, inviting believers to seek his guidance in their spiritual journey. Orthodox Christians pray before these icons, asking for Barnabas's intercession in their growth in faith and understanding. The veneration of Barnabas in this way underscores the role he played as a spiritual teacher and guide, one whose wisdom and dedication to the Gospel continue to influence the lives of the faithful.

In Catholic and Orthodox traditions alike, Barnabas is remembered as a martyr, a title that adds a solemn dimension to his veneration. His willingness to give his life for the faith serves as a powerful example of commitment and courage, inspiring believers to remain steadfast in their convictions. In prayers and devotions that honor his martyrdom, Christians reflect on Barnabas's ultimate sacrifice, asking for the strength to stand firm in their faith even in difficult circumstances. His martyrdom is a reminder of the profound cost of discipleship, a testimony to the depth of his devotion to Christ and the Church.

In modern times, the veneration of Barnabas continues to resonate with believers who seek to embody his virtues in their own lives. His legacy as an encourager, peacemaker, and devoted servant of Christ serves as a source of inspiration for those who wish to live lives of purpose and integrity. Many Christians find in Barnabas a role model who speaks to the challenges of the present day—conflict, division, and the need for unity—and his example offers a way forward through faith, compassion, and understanding.

Barnabas's role as a figure of popular worship highlights the enduring relevance of his life and teachings. Through the ages, he has remained a symbol of hope, courage, and devotion, a man whose life continues to inspire the faithful to reach for higher ideals. His veneration is not just about honoring a saint from the past; it is about embracing the qualities he embodied and allowing his spirit to influence the way believers live, pray, and connect with others.

In honoring Barnabas, Christians are reminded of the power of faith to bring about transformation, to heal divisions, and to inspire unity. His legacy as a beloved apostle and servant of God lives on in the prayers, devotions, and traditions that have been passed down through generations, a testament to the impact he made on the early Church and the Church of today. Through his veneration, Barnabas remains close to the hearts of the faithful, a constant reminder of the strength, grace, and love that define the Christian life. His life calls believers to walk in his footsteps, to live with courage, and to serve others with an open and compassionate heart.

Chapter 33
Ecumenical Relations

Barnabas's legacy as a bridge-builder within the early Church has given him a unique role in the modern ecumenical movement, where his example of unity and inclusivity inspires dialogue among different Christian traditions. From his early days working to bring Gentiles into the Christian fold to his role at the Council of Jerusalem, Barnabas's approach to unity, reconciliation, and mutual respect left a model for fostering harmony. As churches around the world continue to seek common ground and build ecumenical relationships, Barnabas's life and teachings resonate as a source of guidance and encouragement.

In the early Christian community, Barnabas's inclusive approach to faith laid the foundation for a Church that could transcend cultural and ethnic boundaries. His openness to diverse backgrounds and his belief that all people should have access to the Gospel set a precedent for a Church that welcomed both Jews and Gentiles. This inclusive spirit fostered an environment where believers from different cultures could come together in mutual respect, creating a community that transcended social and cultural divides. This legacy is echoed in the ecumenical movement, which aims to unite Christians of varying traditions under the shared commitment to the Gospel and to the teachings of Christ.

Barnabas's role at the Council of Jerusalem was one of his most significant contributions to early ecumenical relations. At the time, the early Church was grappling with the question of whether Gentile converts should be required to follow Jewish customs, a debate that had the potential to create a permanent rift within the Christian community. Barnabas, alongside Paul, argued for the inclusion of Gentiles without imposing the full weight of the Mosaic Law upon them. His advocacy for a Church that welcomed all people, regardless of cultural background, laid the groundwork for a Christian community rooted in unity rather than uniformity. This stance at the Council of Jerusalem set a standard for openness and flexibility in matters of practice, demonstrating that faith in Christ transcended ritual and tradition.

In modern ecumenical efforts, Barnabas is often cited as an example of someone who prioritized unity without compromising on core beliefs. His ability to embrace different perspectives without losing sight of the central message of the Gospel is a quality that ecumenical movements seek to emulate. Churches engaged in ecumenical dialogue look to Barnabas's example of mutual respect, his willingness to advocate for others, and his commitment to maintaining harmony within the Church. His life reminds believers that the pursuit of unity requires not only patience and understanding but also a deep-rooted commitment to the teachings of Christ, which remain the foundation of all Christian traditions.

Barnabas's legacy of ecumenism extends into his role as a mediator and reconciler. In various accounts, he is described as a figure who worked tirelessly to resolve conflicts, both within the Christian community and between the Church and outside groups. His emphasis on reconciliation reflected his belief that division weakens the Church's witness, whereas unity strengthens it. This dedication to reconciliation makes him an enduring symbol for the ecumenical movement, where the goal is to bridge gaps between different Christian denominations and traditions. Barnabas's life shows that unity is not simply a matter of shared doctrine but a commitment to living out the teachings of Christ in ways that bring people together.

Within Catholic, Orthodox, and Protestant traditions, Barnabas is often invoked in ecumenical prayers and gatherings as a model for unity and understanding. Some Christian organizations dedicated to promoting unity hold interdenominational services and conferences on or near his feast day, celebrating his legacy as a figure who brought people together. These gatherings provide a space for believers from different traditions to come together in mutual respect, to pray for greater unity within the body of Christ, and to reflect on the values that bind them together as Christians. In these settings, Barnabas's name and example serve as a reminder of the shared faith that transcends doctrinal differences.

In particular, Barnabas's work with Paul to establish churches that welcomed Gentile converts has resonated with churches in mission-focused ecumenical work. His commitment to an inclusive community mirrors the goals of modern missions that seek to reach people of diverse cultural backgrounds without imposing restrictive customs. His legacy supports the idea that Christianity's message can flourish across cultures, that the faith is expansive enough to encompass a variety of expressions while remaining true to its core. For churches engaged in mission and outreach, Barnabas's example provides a model for embracing diversity and reaching across barriers with compassion and understanding.

Barnabas's ecumenical spirit also lives on in Christian organizations that work toward social justice and humanitarian goals across denominational lines. Inspired by Barnabas's dedication to community and compassion, these organizations often collaborate on initiatives to address issues like poverty, inequality, and conflict, seeing their work as an extension of their shared Christian calling. By working together to serve others, these organizations embody the unity that Barnabas championed, demonstrating that Christians can find common ground in their commitment to love, service, and justice. Barnabas's legacy thus transcends theological boundaries, providing a common example of the call to serve humanity.

In addition to his influence within the Christian community, Barnabas has also become a figure of interfaith dialogue, particularly in regions where Christians live alongside followers of other religions. His reputation as a man of peace, understanding, and inclusivity makes him a model for engaging respectfully with people of different faiths. While Barnabas's primary mission was to spread the Gospel, his interactions with diverse communities reflected a respect for others that resonates with the goals of interfaith dialogue today. His legacy encourages Christians to engage with people of other faiths not as opponents but as neighbors, seeking to build relationships based on respect and understanding.

Modern ecumenical movements also draw inspiration from Barnabas's humility, a trait that allowed him to work effectively alongside others without seeking personal recognition or power. His partnership with Paul demonstrates his willingness to support others in their ministries, even when it meant stepping aside. This humility is essential to ecumenical efforts, where the goal is not to elevate one tradition over another but to seek common ground and mutual support. By embracing humility and respect, Barnabas showed that unity is achieved not through dominance but through a shared commitment to the values of Christ.

In many Christian communities, Barnabas is honored through ecumenical prayers, icons, and celebrations that emphasize his role as a unifier. Some churches hold joint services that include prayers for Barnabas's intercession, asking for his guidance in building relationships across denominational divides. These services often feature readings from scripture that reflect his legacy, such as passages about unity in the body of Christ or about the importance of welcoming others. By coming together in Barnabas's memory, Christians find a shared focus on his example as a guide toward deeper unity and understanding.

Barnabas's life remains a reminder of the importance of placing the mission of Christ above personal or denominational differences. His dedication to the Gospel and his compassion for others provide a timeless example for Christians working to build bridges within the Church. As ecumenical movements seek to foster dialogue, respect, and cooperation, Barnabas's legacy offers both inspiration and guidance, showing that true unity is possible when Christians come together with humility, love, and a commitment to the values they share.

In celebrating Barnabas as a model for ecumenical relations, Christians are invited to reflect on their own role in promoting unity. His life encourages believers to seek out common ground, to build friendships across denominational lines, and to work collaboratively in service to others. Barnabas's legacy challenges the Church to embrace the diversity within its body, to recognize the beauty in each tradition, and to work toward a unity that reflects the love of Christ for all people. Through his example, Christians are reminded that the true strength of the Church lies in its ability to unite in faith, transcending boundaries to create a community that is open, compassionate, and devoted to the Gospel.

Chapter 34
Expansion of Christianity

The legacy of Barnabas extends not only through his personal ministry but through his instrumental role in the expansion of Christianity beyond the confines of Jerusalem and the Jewish community. Known as a man who bridged cultures, Barnabas's commitment to spreading the Gospel created new pathways for Christianity, transforming it from a small sect within Judaism into a faith capable of embracing and influencing diverse populations. His missionary work, vision, and adaptability were central to the Church's growth in the first century, laying foundations for the global nature of Christianity. Barnabas's contributions to this expansion reveal both his deep conviction in the universality of Christ's message and his remarkable ability to connect with people from varied cultural backgrounds.

The Church's expansion began in earnest as Barnabas and Paul embarked on missionary journeys to regions across the Mediterranean, visiting cities and towns where Judaism had already established roots through diaspora communities. Barnabas's cultural sensitivity and his fluency in Hellenistic customs and languages enabled him to connect with both Jews and Gentiles, opening doors to previously unreached populations. In cities like Antioch, where a mix of ethnicities, languages, and beliefs coexisted, Barnabas's inclusive approach resonated with those who had long felt distanced from the religious exclusivity of other faiths. Antioch became one of the first places where Gentiles embraced the Christian faith in large numbers, setting a precedent for the Church's expansion beyond Jewish communities.

Barnabas's work in Antioch is one of the clearest examples of his impact on the spread of Christianity. As a cultural crossroads in the ancient world, Antioch provided fertile ground for a faith capable of transcending cultural boundaries. Barnabas's leadership helped shape this community into a model for the inclusive Church, one that welcomed Gentiles without requiring adherence to Jewish customs. His decision to invite Paul to join him in Antioch underscored his commitment to collaboration, recognizing Paul's potential and the need for strong leaders to guide this growing, diverse congregation. Together, Barnabas and Paul developed a community rooted in love and acceptance, a community where Jews and Gentiles could worship together as equals. Antioch would later become the launching point for many missionary efforts, with its multicultural congregation symbolizing the vision of a universal Church.

As Barnabas and Paul journeyed through regions such as Cyprus, Asia Minor, and Galatia, they encountered varied responses to the message of Christ. In some places, they found open-hearted receptions; in others, resistance and even persecution. Barnabas's adaptability in the face of such diverse reactions allowed him to present the Gospel in ways that resonated with different cultural perspectives. This flexibility did not mean compromising the core message but rather finding ways to communicate it that would speak to people's hearts and minds. His willingness to embrace local customs and his respect for different traditions helped bridge cultural gaps, creating a foundation for a faith that could thrive in any context.

In addition to his adaptability, Barnabas's emphasis on community and mutual support contributed to the spread of Christianity. Wherever he traveled, Barnabas established small communities of believers who met regularly to pray, study scripture, and share in fellowship. These communities provided a support network for new converts, many of whom faced social exclusion or persecution. By establishing strong, interconnected communities, Barnabas created a model of the Church as a supportive family, a place where believers could find belonging and strength. This model would prove essential to the resilience and growth of Christianity, enabling it to flourish even in challenging environments. Barnabas's approach to community-building inspired future generations of missionaries, whose focus on establishing local congregations became a cornerstone of Christian expansion.

One of Barnabas's greatest contributions to the expansion of Christianity was his belief in the Church's mission as a calling for all people, regardless of background. This belief was revolutionary in a time when religion was often tied to ethnicity or nationality. Barnabas's actions and teachings conveyed that the message of Christ was meant for everyone, a radical departure from the sectarianism common in his day. By welcoming Gentiles into the Christian community, Barnabas demonstrated that faith in Christ transcended cultural and religious boundaries, making it possible for Christianity to take root in diverse contexts. His inclusivity helped establish the Church's universal mission, an ideal that would shape its identity for centuries to come.

Barnabas's influence on the expansion of Christianity also extended through his mentorship and encouragement of other leaders. His support for Paul and John Mark not only enriched their individual ministries but also ensured that new leaders would carry forward the mission with the same values of compassion, inclusivity, and unity. By empowering others, Barnabas amplified his impact, allowing the message of Christ to reach farther than he could have accomplished on his own. His example inspired other leaders to invest in mentorship, creating a tradition of discipleship that would become essential to the Church's growth and sustainability. Barnabas's role as a mentor underscored his understanding that the expansion of Christianity required not only evangelism but also the formation of capable and compassionate leaders who would uphold the Church's values.

Throughout his travels, Barnabas demonstrated a resilience that inspired those around him. Faced with opposition, hardship, and the constant challenges of a life on the road, Barnabas's unwavering faith in Christ's message provided strength to his fellow missionaries and to the communities he founded. His resilience became a model for future missionaries, reminding them that the path of faith often involves sacrifice and perseverance. Barnabas's courage in the face of adversity encouraged others to take up the mission, creating a legacy of determination that would fuel the Church's expansion for generations.

Barnabas's contributions to the spread of Christianity are further reflected in his theological openness. His vision of a Church that was inclusive, adaptable, and rooted in the teachings of Christ provided a theological foundation that resonated across cultures. By embracing diversity within the Church, Barnabas encouraged believers to see their differences not as obstacles but as expressions of the Gospel's universality. This openness to theological diversity allowed the Church to engage with new ideas and practices while remaining anchored in its core beliefs. His legacy challenges the Church to continue embracing diversity and adapting to new contexts while maintaining the integrity of its message.

In the centuries following his death, Barnabas's influence on the expansion of Christianity continued to be felt as missionaries, inspired by his example, carried the Gospel to distant lands. His approach to evangelism—grounded in respect, humility, and cultural sensitivity—became a model for future missionaries who sought to share the message of Christ in ways that honored local customs and beliefs. His legacy in mission work reinforced the idea that true evangelism requires empathy, understanding, and a willingness to listen. Barnabas's example inspired generations of missionaries to approach their work with a spirit of compassion and humility, recognizing the dignity of those they sought to reach.

In modern times, Barnabas's role in the expansion of Christianity continues to inspire believers to carry forward the mission of the Church with dedication and love. His life reminds Christians that the Gospel is a message for all people and that the Church's mission is to welcome everyone into a community of faith. His example encourages modern believers to reach out to those who may feel excluded, to build bridges across cultural divides, and to work toward a Church that reflects the universal nature of Christ's love. Barnabas's legacy calls Christians to embrace the global mission of the Church, to see themselves as part of a larger family united by faith, and to carry forward the message of hope and redemption.

Barnabas's contributions to the expansion of Christianity are a testament to the power of faith to bring people together, to transcend boundaries, and to inspire lives of purpose and compassion. His life challenges the Church to continue expanding its reach, to welcome all people with open hearts, and to remain committed to a mission that spans cultures, languages, and generations. Through his example, Barnabas invites believers to become agents of Christ's love in the world, to carry forward the message of salvation, and to build a Church that is as wide and inclusive as God's grace.

The legacy of Barnabas in the expansion of Christianity endures as a reminder that the mission of the Church is a calling for all believers. His life and work inspire Christians to see themselves as part of a global movement, a family bound together by faith in Christ and by a shared commitment to spread the Gospel. Through his example, Barnabas calls each believer to embrace their role in the mission, to work toward a Church that reflects the beauty of its diversity, and to carry forward the message of love and unity that defined his life and his ministry.

Chapter 35
Historical Controversies

Barnabas's life and legacy, like those of many influential figures, have been marked by historical controversies that reveal the complexities of his role in the early Church. While he is revered as an apostle and pioneer in the spread of Christianity, certain aspects of his life and teachings have sparked debate and conflicting interpretations. From his association with the apocryphal *Gospel of Barnabas* to the controversies surrounding his separation from Paul, the figure of Barnabas presents a fascinating blend of inspiration and mystery. These historical controversies add depth to his legacy, inviting believers to engage with the complexities of early Christianity and the nuances of Barnabas's contributions to the faith.

One of the most well-known controversies involving Barnabas centers around the *Gospel of Barnabas*, an apocryphal text that claims to narrate the life of Jesus through Barnabas's perspective. This text, however, is widely believed by scholars to have been written centuries after Barnabas's lifetime, and it contains theological views and historical anachronisms inconsistent with early Christian doctrine. The *Gospel of Barnabas* portrays a version of Jesus that diverges from canonical teachings, aligning instead with some aspects of Islamic beliefs. This portrayal, combined with linguistic and stylistic analysis, has led scholars to conclude that the text was likely written in the Middle Ages, possibly as a tool for interfaith dialogue between Christians and Muslims. Despite its doubtful authenticity, the *Gospel of Barnabas* has been a source of controversy, raising questions about Barnabas's role as an apostolic figure and about the boundaries of early Christian thought.

The existence of the *Gospel of Barnabas* has fueled a variety of interpretations over the centuries. Some readers have viewed the text as a lost gospel that reveals hidden truths about Jesus, while others have dismissed it as a later fabrication with no connection to the historical Barnabas. This controversy highlights the complexities of early Christian literature, where canonical and non-canonical texts circulated alongside each other, shaping and challenging beliefs within the community. For scholars and believers alike, the *Gospel of Barnabas* serves as a reminder of the fluidity of early Christian literature and the importance of discernment in distinguishing between authentic teachings and later additions. This controversy invites Christians to engage critically with historical sources, to seek knowledge and understanding, and to recognize that the development of Christian doctrine was a complex process that required careful examination of diverse perspectives.

Another significant controversy surrounding Barnabas involves his separation from Paul, an event that has sparked considerable debate among theologians and historians. The rift occurred during their second missionary journey, when Barnabas wanted to bring John Mark along, despite his earlier abandonment of a mission. Paul, however, disagreed, leading to a sharp disagreement between the two apostles that resulted in their parting ways. This conflict has been interpreted in various ways, with some viewing it as a reflection of differing leadership styles or priorities, while others see it as a necessary step that allowed each apostle to pursue his calling in separate but complementary ways. For many, the parting of Barnabas and Paul raises questions about unity, forgiveness, and the nature of disagreement within the Church.

The separation between Barnabas and Paul can be seen as both a challenge and a testament to the human dynamics within the early Church. While the incident reflects a moment of tension, it also underscores the complexity of maintaining unity among diverse personalities and perspectives. Some theologians argue that Barnabas's decision to support John Mark, even at the cost of his partnership with Paul, highlights his deep commitment to forgiveness and second chances. Barnabas's loyalty to John Mark suggests a belief in growth and redemption, values that would later bear fruit as John Mark became a valuable contributor to the early Church. The controversy surrounding this separation invites reflection on the balance between unity and individuality, reminding believers that even the earliest apostles faced challenges in maintaining harmony while pursuing their distinct missions.

The divergent paths of Barnabas and Paul have also sparked discussion about leadership styles within the Church. Barnabas's compassionate and inclusive approach contrasts with Paul's more rigorous and mission-driven style, illustrating the diversity of approaches that can coexist within the faith. This contrast reflects the broader question of how different leadership styles and priorities contribute to the Church's mission. For some, Barnabas represents a model of relational leadership, one that prioritizes mentorship, encouragement, and personal support. His disagreement with Paul underscores the reality that different perspectives can both serve the Church, offering complementary strengths that enhance its overall mission. This controversy invites the Church to value diverse forms of leadership, recognizing that each approach brings unique gifts to the faith community.

The historical record on Barnabas also includes ambiguity regarding his martyrdom, with various sources offering differing accounts of the circumstances surrounding his death. While tradition holds that he was martyred in Cyprus, some accounts vary in their descriptions of the exact location and manner of his death. These discrepancies have led to questions about the reliability of certain sources and the extent to which later hagiography shaped the narrative of Barnabas's martyrdom. The ambiguity surrounding his death highlights the challenges of reconstructing the lives of early Christian figures, many of whom left limited historical records. This uncertainty invites believers to approach historical sources with both reverence and critical thinking, acknowledging the role of tradition while remaining open to the complexities of history.

Another area of controversy involves Barnabas's role in early theological debates, particularly in relation to the inclusion of Gentiles. Barnabas's advocacy for the Gentile mission was groundbreaking, but it also placed him in the midst of significant theological tensions. His stance at the Council of Jerusalem, where he argued against imposing Jewish customs on Gentile converts, reflected a progressive view that challenged the traditional beliefs of many Jewish Christians. This position created tensions within the early Church, as some believers struggled to reconcile their Jewish heritage with the emerging identity of Christianity. Barnabas's role in this debate reflects the growing pains of a movement that was expanding beyond its cultural roots. His advocacy for Gentile inclusion helped to shape the Church's identity, but it also generated resistance and debate among those who held different theological perspectives.

This controversy over the inclusion of Gentiles raises broader questions about identity, tradition, and change within the Church. Barnabas's vision of a faith that could embrace diverse backgrounds without requiring conformity to specific cultural practices challenged the early Church to reimagine its boundaries and to consider what it meant to be part of the Christian community. His stance in this debate underscores the dynamic nature of early Christianity, a movement that was constantly evolving in response to new ideas, experiences, and cultural influences. Barnabas's advocacy for inclusivity invites the Church to continue embracing diversity, to remain open to growth, and to navigate the tensions that arise from adapting to new contexts while honoring tradition.

The controversies surrounding Barnabas also reveal the complexity of his legacy and the ways in which his life continues to inspire debate and reflection. His association with the apocryphal *Gospel of Barnabas*, his separation from Paul, the ambiguity of his martyrdom, and his role in theological debates all contribute to a portrait of Barnabas as a multifaceted figure whose influence is felt both within and beyond the Church. These controversies invite believers to engage with his legacy in a spirit of curiosity and respect, to seek understanding of the historical context in which he lived, and to recognize that the development of Christian identity was a process shaped by diverse voices and perspectives.

For modern Christians, the controversies surrounding Barnabas offer valuable insights into the nature of faith and the complexity of religious leadership. His life reminds believers that the journey of faith often involves navigating uncertainties, embracing diversity, and grappling with difficult questions. Barnabas's willingness to challenge established norms, to stand up for inclusivity, and to pursue reconciliation even in the face of disagreement reflects a commitment to a faith that is both resilient and compassionate. His legacy challenges the Church to approach controversies not as obstacles but as opportunities for growth, reflection, and deeper understanding.

In the end, the historical controversies associated with Barnabas add depth and richness to his legacy, inviting believers to explore the complexities of his life with open hearts and minds. His example encourages Christians to remain steadfast in their convictions while being open to dialogue, to seek unity without sacrificing individual integrity, and to engage with the evolving nature of faith. Through the lens of these controversies, Barnabas emerges not as a figure of simple certainties but as a dynamic and complex apostle whose life continues to inspire and challenge the Church to this day.

Chapter 36
Manuscripts and Historical Documents

The legacy of Barnabas endures not only in the traditions and teachings of the Church but also in the manuscripts and historical documents that preserve his life and contributions. From early Christian writings and canonical scriptures to ancient texts and later apocryphal works, these documents reveal glimpses of Barnabas's role in the early Church and offer insights into the faith of the communities he helped to shape. They also highlight the evolution of Barnabas's image through time, as subsequent generations interpreted and reinterpreted his life in ways that reflected their own theological concerns and spiritual ideals. The preservation of these manuscripts underscores Barnabas's enduring influence and the importance of historical documentation in understanding the foundations of Christianity.

The canonical New Testament, particularly the Book of Acts and the Pauline Epistles, contains the earliest references to Barnabas, providing invaluable historical context and shaping his legacy as a significant figure in the early Church. In Acts, Barnabas is portrayed as a respected leader, a man "full of the Holy Spirit and faith" who played a crucial role in bridging cultural divides and fostering unity between Jewish and Gentile believers. His mentorship of Paul, his work in Antioch, and his missionary journeys provide the foundational narrative of his life, painting a picture of a devoted apostle committed to spreading the Gospel. The New Testament documents also provide details about Barnabas's personality—his generosity, his role as an encourager, and his commitment to reconciliation—all of which have contributed to his enduring image in Christian tradition.

In addition to the canonical accounts, early Christian writers such as Clement of Alexandria and Eusebius of Caesarea referenced Barnabas in their works, further cementing his role in the history of the Church. These early Church Fathers often portrayed Barnabas as a model of faith, piety, and humility. Eusebius, a notable historian of the early Church, included Barnabas in his writings, emphasizing his influence in spreading Christianity and his role as one of the first apostles to preach to the Gentiles. Through the writings of these Church Fathers, Barnabas's image as a revered figure continued to grow, serving as an example of dedication to God and to the mission of the Church. These early references not only preserved Barnabas's memory but also offered the faithful a figure to emulate, reinforcing his legacy as a pillar of the early Christian community.

One of the most intriguing manuscripts associated with Barnabas is the apocryphal *Epistle of Barnabas*, a text that was widely read and respected in some early Christian communities, though it was ultimately excluded from the New Testament canon. Traditionally attributed to Barnabas, this letter offers a unique perspective on early Christian thought, interpreting the Old Testament in a way that foreshadows New Testament themes. The *Epistle of Barnabas* uses an allegorical approach, reinterpreting Jewish rituals and symbols as representations of Christian beliefs. For example, it views the concept of circumcision as a metaphor for the transformation of the heart rather than a physical practice, reflecting the spiritualization of Jewish customs within early Christian theology.

The *Epistle of Barnabas* has been both influential and controversial, as its interpretation of scripture differs from traditional Jewish readings and reflects a shift toward a distinctly Christian identity. Although not written by Barnabas himself, the text embodies the values he championed, such as faith over ritual and the importance of spiritual transformation. The document's exclusion from the canon does not diminish its significance; rather, it serves as a valuable artifact that illustrates the diversity of early Christian thought. Its themes of grace, faith, and the reinterpretation of the Law continue to offer insights into the ways early Christians sought to understand their relationship with God and the world.

Another apocryphal text, the *Acts of Barnabas*, attributed to John Mark, adds to the collection of manuscripts that sought to preserve the apostle's life and teachings. Although its historical accuracy is debated, this text offers an account of Barnabas's missionary work, his interactions with various communities, and his eventual martyrdom. It describes his preaching in Cyprus and his opposition to paganism, framing his life as a series of encounters where faith overcame resistance. The *Acts of Barnabas* also includes details about his final days, portraying his martyrdom as a testament to his unwavering dedication to the Gospel. This narrative, though later and likely embellished, reflects the admiration that Barnabas inspired among early Christians, who saw in him a model of courage and steadfastness.

In addition to these manuscripts, the preservation of Barnabas's legacy can be seen in the various church councils and theological debates that referenced his contributions. The Council of Jerusalem, recounted in Acts, provides one of the most direct examples of his influence, as Barnabas advocated for the inclusion of Gentiles without requiring them to follow the entirety of Jewish law. This decision had lasting theological implications, shaping the early Church's approach to inclusivity and its understanding of faith as the basis of salvation. The decisions and discussions of this council, preserved in canonical scripture, highlight Barnabas's role as a bridge-builder, whose contributions set precedents for the Church's growth and unity.

Historical documents also reveal the process by which Barnabas's image evolved over time, as different Christian traditions highlighted various aspects of his life and teachings. In some manuscripts, Barnabas is presented as a model of humility and generosity, emphasizing his decision to sell his property for the benefit of the community. Other documents, especially those written during times of persecution, focus on his courage and willingness to endure suffering for the sake of Christ. The varying portrayals of Barnabas across historical documents reflect the ways in which each generation of Christians found inspiration in his life, adapting his legacy to meet their own spiritual and cultural needs.

The preservation of relics and manuscripts connected to Barnabas also played a significant role in maintaining his legacy. According to tradition, Barnabas's remains were discovered in Cyprus in the fifth century, along with a copy of the Gospel of Matthew said to have been placed on his chest. This discovery sparked renewed interest in Barnabas's life and led to the construction of churches and monasteries in his honor. Manuscripts recounting the discovery of these relics helped to solidify Barnabas's status as a beloved apostle and martyr, reinforcing his importance in the devotional life of the Church. The veneration of his relics, along with the preservation of manuscripts about his life, created a lasting connection between Barnabas and the communities that honored him.

In addition to these ancient documents, later Christian scholars and historians continued to study and write about Barnabas, preserving and expanding upon earlier accounts. Renaissance theologians, inspired by the rediscovery of classical texts and the humanist movement, revisited the works of early Church Fathers and apocryphal texts, shedding new light on figures like Barnabas. These scholars analyzed the historical context of Barnabas's life, examining his influence on the early Church and exploring the theological implications of his teachings. This renewed scholarly interest preserved Barnabas's legacy for future generations and contributed to a more nuanced understanding of his role in Christian history.

Modern historians and theologians continue to examine the manuscripts and historical documents associated with Barnabas, using these texts to understand the formation of early Christian identity, theology, and community structure. These studies provide valuable insights into the social, cultural, and theological dynamics of the first-century Church, illustrating the challenges and triumphs of those who spread the Gospel in its earliest days. By examining these documents, scholars gain a deeper understanding of the foundational beliefs and practices that defined Christianity's formative years, as well as the ways in which Barnabas and his contemporaries shaped the future of the faith.

The historical documents connected to Barnabas offer a complex and layered portrait of a man whose life and ministry continue to inspire and challenge believers. Through canonical texts, apocryphal writings, council records, and accounts of his relics, the legacy of Barnabas emerges as one of enduring influence and spiritual depth. These manuscripts and documents serve as windows into the past, allowing modern readers to engage with the world of the early Church and to encounter the faith and resilience of those who first carried the message of Christ.

In honoring the manuscripts and historical documents that preserve Barnabas's legacy, the Church acknowledges the importance of memory and historical continuity in the life of faith. These documents remind believers of the sacrifices, insights, and dedication that shaped the Christian tradition and inspire them to continue the work of those who went before. Through these preserved writings, the spirit of Barnabas lives on, a reminder of the transformative power of faith, the richness of Christian history, and the enduring call to spread the Gospel with courage, compassion, and humility.

Chapter 37
Legends and Popular Narratives

The life and legacy of Barnabas have given rise to a rich tapestry of legends and popular narratives that add depth and color to the story of this early apostle. These tales, though often rooted in kernels of historical truth, blend fact and fiction in ways that reveal the devotion and imagination of the communities that cherished his memory. Legends surrounding Barnabas capture the qualities he embodied—faith, compassion, courage—and expand upon them, often highlighting miraculous events, supernatural acts, and interactions with both the faithful and skeptics. These popular narratives, passed down through generations, underscore the impact of Barnabas on the Christian imagination, transforming his life into stories of inspiration and wonder that reach beyond the historical record.

One of the most enduring legends associated with Barnabas is the story of his martyrdom in Cyprus. Tradition holds that Barnabas returned to Cyprus, his homeland, to continue his missionary work in the later years of his life. According to the legend, his success in converting many Cypriots to Christianity provoked the ire of local religious authorities and pagan leaders, who saw his influence as a threat to their own power. Enraged by his growing following, they ultimately arrested and stoned him to death. While historical records about Barnabas's death are sparse, this account of martyrdom became an enduring part of his legacy, painting him as a steadfast figure who faced persecution with unshakable faith. This narrative of martyrdom not only inspired early Christians in times of trial but also served as a powerful reminder of the sacrifices made by those who spread the Gospel.

Accompanying the story of Barnabas's martyrdom is the tale of the miraculous discovery of his tomb. According to legend, Barnabas's remains were lost for several centuries until they were rediscovered in the fifth century. The story goes that Bishop Anthemios of Cyprus experienced a vision in which Barnabas appeared to him, revealing the location of his burial site. Following the vision, Anthemios led an excavation that uncovered a tomb containing Barnabas's remains, with a copy of the Gospel of Matthew lying on his chest. This miraculous discovery of Barnabas's tomb was seen as a divine affirmation of his sainthood and led to the establishment of Cyprus as an autocephalous, or self-governing, Church. The legend surrounding the discovery of Barnabas's tomb became a cherished story within the Cypriot Christian community, reinforcing his status as a beloved apostle and protector of the island.

Another popular narrative about Barnabas revolves around his relationship with John Mark, the young man who accompanied him and Paul on their first missionary journey. According to tradition, Barnabas and John Mark's bond went beyond that of mentor and disciple; some accounts suggest they were cousins, making Barnabas's decision to advocate for John Mark after his desertion all the more poignant. The legend portrays Barnabas as a compassionate figure who believed in second chances and saw the potential for growth in John Mark, despite his earlier failings. This story of redemption and reconciliation has resonated deeply with believers, presenting Barnabas as a model of forgiveness and understanding. His faith in John Mark became a symbolic reminder of the Church's mission to nurture those who falter, a message that has been preserved and cherished through popular narrative.

Legends also credit Barnabas with performing numerous miracles during his lifetime, particularly during his travels through Cyprus and Asia Minor. One popular story recounts how

Barnabas encountered a man possessed by an evil spirit. Barnabas, moved by compassion, is said to have prayed fervently, casting out the spirit and freeing the man from his torment. This miraculous act became a testament to Barnabas's spiritual power and deep connection with the Holy Spirit, a narrative that encouraged believers to seek his intercession for healing and protection. Tales of such miracles highlight the image of Barnabas not only as a preacher and teacher but as a channel of divine grace, an apostle through whom God's presence was made manifest in powerful and tangible ways.

In addition to stories of physical healings, Barnabas is also remembered in legends for his ability to bring peace and reconciliation to divided communities. One tale recounts how, during his travels, Barnabas entered a village embroiled in a bitter dispute. Seeing the division among the people, Barnabas called them together, speaking to them about the teachings of Christ on forgiveness and unity. Through his words and prayers, the village found common ground, and peace was restored. This narrative reflects Barnabas's reputation as a peacemaker, a man whose influence brought healing not only to individuals but to entire communities. Such stories reinforce his legacy as a symbol of harmony and remind believers of the transformative power of kindness and empathy.

One particularly beloved legend tells of Barnabas's intervention during a time of drought in Cyprus. According to this story, Barnabas, seeing the suffering of the people, prayed for rain, asking God to relieve their hardship. Miraculously, rain began to fall, ending the drought and restoring the land's fertility. This tale of divine intercession portrays Barnabas as an advocate for the well-being of his homeland and a man deeply attuned to the needs of his people. For the people of Cyprus, this story solidified Barnabas's role as a patron and protector, a figure they could turn to in times of difficulty. The legend of the rain prayer endures as a cherished part of Cypriot Christian tradition, reinforcing Barnabas's close connection to the island and its people.

Beyond these miracles and intercessions, stories about Barnabas often emphasize his wisdom and patience in teaching. In popular narratives, Barnabas is depicted as a kind and approachable teacher, someone who could explain complex spiritual truths in ways that everyone could understand. One such tale tells of a young skeptic who challenged Barnabas's teachings. Rather than dismissing the young man, Barnabas engaged him in dialogue, patiently addressing his questions and doubts. By the end of their conversation, the young man was so moved by Barnabas's kindness and insight that he converted to Christianity. This portrayal of Barnabas as a gentle and wise teacher has endured as a source of inspiration, encouraging believers to approach others with patience and compassion, especially those who may doubt or struggle in their faith.

In addition to these individual tales, the legacy of Barnabas has woven itself into larger folk traditions in various Christian cultures. In Cyprus, his feast day on June 11 is often marked by special services, processions, and community celebrations. These gatherings honor Barnabas's role as the island's patron saint and protector, providing an opportunity for people to remember his life, celebrate his miracles, and seek his blessings. Folk customs associated with his feast day include prayers for protection, blessings of homes and fields, and acts of charity, all reflecting the values of faith, compassion, and generosity that defined Barnabas's life. Through these traditions, Barnabas's legacy continues to be a living presence in the lives of the faithful.

Barnabas's legendary status also extends beyond the Christian world; in interfaith contexts, his image as a compassionate and inclusive figure has made him a bridge between different religious traditions. Stories of Barnabas's dedication to peace and unity have resonated with people of various faiths, who see in him a figure of moral integrity and spiritual openness. In regions where Christians, Jews, and Muslims have historically coexisted, the figure of Barnabas is sometimes referenced as a symbol of shared values, an apostle who embodied the principles of respect and understanding. This interfaith dimension of his legacy highlights the universal appeal of his character, a testament to the timeless qualities of love, humility, and compassion that transcend religious boundaries.

The legends and popular narratives about Barnabas reveal not only the qualities that endeared him to the early Church but also the ways in which his life has continued to inspire generations. These stories, though they may not always align with historical fact, capture the essence of Barnabas's spirit and the impact he had on those around him. They invite believers to see beyond the limitations of history and to embrace the larger truths that his life represents—faith that moves mountains, compassion that heals, and wisdom that unites. Through these stories, Barnabas remains a beloved figure, a source of inspiration for those who seek to live lives of faith, kindness, and courage.

In honoring the legends of Barnabas, the Church celebrates the enduring power of storytelling to convey spiritual truths and to inspire lives of devotion. These popular narratives remind believers that faith is not only about doctrine but about embodying the virtues that define the Christian life. Through the tales of his miracles, his teachings, and his compassion, Barnabas's legacy lives on, inviting each new generation to find meaning, inspiration, and hope in his story.

Chapter 38
Patron of Specific Causes

In the centuries following his life and ministry, Barnabas became associated with various causes and professions, earning him a place of special honor in the hearts of those who look to him for protection, guidance, and intercession. Revered as a peacemaker, encourager, and compassionate healer, Barnabas embodies qualities that resonate with people across different fields and life circumstances. His legacy as a patron saint reflects the spiritual and moral values he championed, allowing believers to draw on his example as they seek strength, guidance, and support in their own challenges.

One of the most significant causes for which Barnabas is invoked is as a patron of peace and reconciliation. His role as a mediator within the early Church and his dedication to bringing unity among believers created a lasting image of him as a peacemaker. Barnabas's support for the inclusion of Gentiles, his reconciliation with John Mark, and his commitment to fostering harmony in the Christian community have made him an enduring symbol of peace. Christians who work in fields of mediation, conflict resolution, and diplomacy often look to Barnabas as a model, drawing on his example of humility, understanding, and patience. In prayer, they seek his intercession for wisdom and guidance in their efforts to bring peace and understanding to divided communities, seeing in him a spiritual mentor for their vocation.

Barnabas is also venerated as a patron of encouragement, offering hope and strength to those who struggle with doubt, discouragement, or difficult circumstances. Known as the "son of encouragement," Barnabas's gift for lifting others' spirits and his ability to inspire confidence in their potential have made him a powerful figure for those who seek support in challenging times. People facing personal or professional trials, as well as those who dedicate their lives to uplifting others—such as counselors, mentors, and teachers—often pray to Barnabas for the strength to inspire and encourage others. His legacy as an encourager reminds believers that faith in God can empower them to face life's difficulties with resilience and hope, and his example provides a source of comfort for those seeking the courage to persevere.

In addition to his association with peace and encouragement, Barnabas is recognized as a patron of healing. Throughout his life, he demonstrated compassion for the suffering, and various accounts tell of his healing touch. Though the historical details of these miracles are uncertain, the image of Barnabas as a healer has inspired generations to seek his intercession for physical, emotional, and spiritual healing. Many healthcare workers, particularly those involved in caring professions, regard Barnabas as a protector and source of inspiration. They pray to him for guidance and strength in their work, seeing him as a figure who embodied both the skill and compassion required to care for others. Patients and those suffering from illness or injury also turn to Barnabas, asking for his intercession and the strength to endure their suffering with faith.

Barnabas's legacy of compassion extends to those working in social service and charity. His act of selling his property to support the needs of the early Christian community exemplifies his commitment to generosity and solidarity with the less fortunate. Social workers, charitable organizations, and advocates for the marginalized often look to Barnabas as a patron of charity, drawing inspiration from his selflessness and dedication to serving others. His life encourages them to continue their work with compassion, humility, and a sense of shared responsibility for the welfare of all people. Through prayers and acts of devotion, they seek his intercession to guide their efforts and to inspire others to live lives of generosity and service.

Barnabas's journey as a missionary, his dedication to spreading the Gospel, and his willingness to face hardship for his faith have made him a patron of missionaries and evangelists. Those who embark on missionary work, often in unfamiliar and challenging environments, find in Barnabas a model of courage, adaptability, and commitment to God's call. Missionaries pray to Barnabas for protection, strength, and resilience as they share the message of Christ with others. His life reminds them that true evangelism requires both faith and empathy, an openness to diverse cultures and a respect for the dignity of all people. Barnabas's example as a missionary has inspired countless individuals to approach their work with patience, kindness, and an unwavering dedication to spreading the Gospel.

Artists, particularly those inspired by faith, also look to Barnabas as a patron. His encouragement of others, his openness to different perspectives, and his capacity to inspire resonate deeply with those who see art as a form of spiritual expression. Artists seeking creativity, guidance, or inspiration may pray to Barnabas, asking for his intercession to help them create works that uplift and connect with others on a spiritual level. Barnabas's influence in this area reflects his legacy as an encourager, someone whose life exemplifies the power of creativity and the importance of fostering beauty and meaning in the world.

Barnabas's role as a mentor has also made him a patron for those involved in education and mentorship. Teachers, professors, and mentors see in Barnabas a model of patient guidance, someone who brought out the best in those around him, such as his young protégé John Mark. His mentorship of John Mark, despite earlier disappointments, stands as an enduring example of the transformative power of second chances. Educators and mentors pray to Barnabas for wisdom and patience, seeking his intercession to help them inspire, guide, and nurture their students. His example reminds them of the impact that compassionate and dedicated mentorship can have on future generations.

In Cyprus, where Barnabas is particularly venerated, he is regarded as a protector and patron of the island. His legacy as the apostle who first brought Christianity to Cyprus has left a profound impact on its culture, traditions, and spiritual life. Cypriots turn to Barnabas as a source of guidance and protection, particularly in times of hardship or conflict. His intercession is sought not only for personal needs but for the well-being and peace of the entire island. Cypriot Christians celebrate Barnabas's feast day with special prayers, services, and processions, honoring him as both a national and spiritual guardian. His legacy in Cyprus exemplifies his role as a regional patron and highlights the lasting impact of his missionary work on the island's faith and identity.

For those working in fields that involve challenging social or moral decisions, such as law and public service, Barnabas is seen as a patron of integrity and moral courage. His commitment to inclusivity and justice within the early Church, along with his role in advocating for the rights of Gentile converts, reflects a deep-seated belief in the dignity and equality of all people. Lawmakers, advocates, and leaders pray to Barnabas for guidance in making ethical decisions, seeking his intercession to remain true to their values and to act with justice and compassion. His legacy encourages those in positions of influence to serve the common good and to approach their responsibilities with humility and integrity.

Finally, Barnabas's dedication to bridging divides within the early Christian community has made him a patron for those involved in ecumenical and interfaith work. His life exemplifies the importance of unity, understanding, and respect among diverse communities. Those who work to foster dialogue and collaboration among different Christian denominations, as well as those engaged in interfaith initiatives, see Barnabas as a guiding figure. His role in advocating for the inclusion of Gentiles and his ability to reconcile differing perspectives inspire them to seek common ground and to build bridges of mutual respect. Through his intercession, they pray for wisdom and courage to overcome divisions and to promote a spirit of unity in the shared pursuit of peace and understanding.

Barnabas's role as a patron of these diverse causes reveals the breadth of his impact and the enduring relevance of his life. His qualities—compassion, courage, humility, and dedication—are virtues that transcend time and place, speaking to the hearts of those who seek to live lives of faith and service. The causes associated with Barnabas reflect his mission to spread love, peace, and hope, making him a model for believers who strive to make a positive impact on the world.

Through prayers, devotions, and acts of service, those who look to Barnabas as a patron continue to draw strength from his example. His life challenges Christians to embody the qualities he lived, to bring hope to those in need, and to approach every aspect of life as an opportunity to serve God and others. As a patron of peace, encouragement, healing, mentorship, and more, Barnabas's legacy invites believers to walk in his footsteps, to be voices of encouragement, and to shine the light of Christ into the world. His life serves as a reminder that each person's actions, however small, can contribute to a larger mission of love, unity, and compassion.

Chapter 39
Interpretations During the Reformation and Counter-Reformation

During the Reformation and Counter-Reformation, Barnabas's legacy took on new layers of interpretation, reflecting the intense theological debates and shifting dynamics of 16th- and 17th-century Christianity. As Protestant reformers challenged the authority, traditions, and doctrines of the Catholic Church, and as the Catholic Church responded with its own internal reforms, figures from the early Christian period like Barnabas were reevaluated to serve new ideological and theological purposes. This era of intense religious transformation brought Barnabas's life, writings, and legacy into fresh focus as both sides of the Reformation sought to interpret his contributions in ways that supported their distinct theological visions and goals.

For Protestant reformers, the early Church, especially its first apostles and missionaries, represented an ideal of unadulterated Christianity—a time before the institution of the Church became, in their view, overly hierarchical and corrupt. In this context, Barnabas was seen as a figure who embodied qualities that reformers valued: humility, simplicity, dedication to the Gospel, and a rejection of material wealth. His sale of his property to benefit the community, recorded in Acts, resonated with reformers who believed that Christianity should reject materialism and embrace a more communal and austere way of life. Protestant interpretations of Barnabas highlighted his selflessness and his commitment to the Gospel, holding him up as an example of a life focused entirely on faith rather than wealth or power.

Moreover, Protestant reformers valued Barnabas's role as a missionary, someone who spread the Gospel not through elaborate rituals but through personal witness, prayer, and scripture. His straightforward approach to preaching Christ's message, especially in his missionary journeys, was celebrated by those who sought a return to what they saw as the purity of the early Church. Barnabas's willingness to travel, face hardship, and engage with diverse cultures spoke to the reformers' desire to reclaim the simplicity of apostolic Christianity. His partnership with Paul was interpreted as a model of collaborative ministry and was used to support Protestant ideas about shared pastoral work and the mutuality of Christian leadership, in contrast to the centralized authority of the Catholic Church.

The figure of Barnabas was also invoked in discussions around the inclusion of scripture and the authority of religious texts. Reformers, who advocated for "sola scriptura" (scripture alone) as the guiding principle of faith, often cited early Christian texts, both canonical and apocryphal, to support their views on the Bible's central role. Barnabas's association with early Christian writings, especially the apocryphal *Epistle of Barnabas*, brought him into these debates. Though the epistle was not included in the canon, its existence provided reformers with an example of early Christian texts that did not align with later Church doctrines and practices. The *Epistle of Barnabas*, with its focus on moral and allegorical teachings, served as an example of a simpler, more direct approach to faith that resonated with Protestant ideals.

Catholic interpretations of Barnabas during the Counter-Reformation, however, took a different approach, emphasizing his role as a unifier and advocate for Church authority. In the face of the Reformation's challenges to Catholic structure and tradition, Catholic theologians turned to figures like Barnabas as symbols of the Church's continuity, apostolic authority, and unbroken tradition. Barnabas's close association with Paul, one of the Church's foundational apostles, highlighted his support of a unified Church and reinforced the idea of an apostolic chain that led directly to the Catholic hierarchy. For the Catholic Church, Barnabas's legacy supported the notion of a cohesive Church body guided by leaders who were empowered to preserve doctrine and safeguard the faith.

Catholic scholars emphasized Barnabas's role in the Council of Jerusalem, where he supported the inclusion of Gentiles while respecting the authority of the apostles in making doctrinal decisions. This stance was seen as a model for respectful theological dialogue and ecclesiastical order. In a time when Protestant reformers were calling for a decentralized, scripture-focused faith, the Catholic Church viewed Barnabas's actions as proof that doctrinal development required a unified Church with clear authority to make binding decisions. His participation in the Council underscored the Catholic teaching that Church councils and apostolic authority were essential for preserving true Christian doctrine across generations.

In addition to promoting Barnabas as a figure of Church unity, Catholic theologians also highlighted his virtues of humility and service. His decision to sell his possessions and give to the community was interpreted as evidence of the Catholic values of charity and communal support. The Counter-Reformation, which sought to renew the moral and spiritual integrity of the Catholic Church, found in Barnabas a model of self-sacrifice and dedication to communal welfare. His actions served as an ideal for clergy and laypeople alike, reminding Catholics of the importance of charity, humility, and commitment to the Church's mission.

The Reformation period also saw a renewed interest in apocryphal texts, which brought both Protestant and Catholic perspectives on Barnabas's possible authorship of the *Epistle of Barnabas* into focus. Though neither side accepted the epistle as canonical, its themes were discussed in light of the theological issues of the day. For reformers, the epistle's focus on moral purity and its symbolic interpretation of the Old Testament resonated with their critique of ritualistic practices. For Catholics, while the text was acknowledged as non-canonical, its existence was used to highlight the early diversity of Christian writings and the necessity of an authoritative Church to discern orthodoxy. The epistle's allegorical interpretations of Old Testament customs, such as circumcision as a symbol of spiritual purity, inspired discussions on the boundaries of doctrinal interpretation, fueling the era's debates over scriptural interpretation and authority.

In the art and literature of the Reformation and Counter-Reformation periods, Barnabas was often depicted as a figure of strength and dedication, reflecting each side's view of his role in the early Church. Protestant art sometimes emphasized Barnabas's missionary journeys, portraying him as a humble traveler and preacher, a man of faith who spread the Gospel without relying on Church structures. This imagery supported the Protestant view of a more egalitarian Christianity, rooted in scripture and accessible to all believers. Catholic art, by contrast, often depicted Barnabas in the context of his partnership with Paul or his role in the Council of Jerusalem, emphasizing his commitment to unity and his adherence to apostolic authority. These portrayals reinforced the Catholic perspective of Barnabas as a man who respected ecclesiastical order and contributed to the Church's mission through cooperation with established leadership.

In both Protestant and Catholic traditions, Barnabas's role as an encourager and supporter was widely recognized, inspiring believers to see him as a model of Christian charity and compassion. His relationship with John Mark, particularly his decision to give the young disciple a second chance despite past failures, resonated with both sides as a model of mercy and forgiveness. This aspect of Barnabas's life transcended the theological divides of the era, reminding Christians of the importance of kindness, patience, and belief in the potential of others. His mentorship of John Mark provided both Protestants and Catholics with a narrative that underscored the universal values of compassion and faith, showing that even in times of division, Christians could find common ground in the teachings of love and encouragement.

As the Reformation and Counter-Reformation unfolded, the interpretation of Barnabas's life and legacy became a mirror reflecting the distinct visions and ideals of these competing Christian traditions. For Protestants, he was a model of simplicity, humility, and a return to apostolic roots, a figure who exemplified the values of a reformed Christianity grounded in scripture and personal faith. For Catholics, Barnabas represented unity, loyalty to the apostolic mission, and the importance of Church authority, serving as an example of faithfulness to the communal and hierarchical structure of the Church.

In modern times, the varied interpretations of Barnabas that emerged during the Reformation and Counter-Reformation continue to enrich his legacy, reminding believers of the diverse ways in which his life can speak to the challenges and aspirations of different eras. His life invites Christians to embrace humility, to seek unity while respecting diversity, and to follow Christ with courage and compassion. Through the lens of both Protestant and Catholic perspectives, Barnabas's legacy continues to inspire a Church that, though historically divided, remains united in its reverence for the virtues he exemplified.

Chapter 40
Archaeological Discoveries

Archaeological discoveries related to Barnabas and the early Christian communities he helped establish have provided valuable insights into the historical context of his ministry and the legacy he left behind. These findings, including ancient churches, artifacts, and burial sites, offer a glimpse into the lives of early Christians and allow historians to connect the narrative of Barnabas's ministry with tangible remains. While archaeological evidence is often limited in scope, each discovery contributes to a more nuanced understanding of Barnabas's impact and sheds light on the early spread of Christianity. These relics and ruins remind believers and historians alike of the profound ways in which Barnabas and his fellow apostles shaped the ancient world, leaving a legacy that continues to resonate through the centuries.

One of the most significant archaeological sites associated with Barnabas is located on the island of Cyprus, where he is believed to have spent his final years. Tradition holds that Barnabas was martyred in Cyprus around 61 AD and that his remains were buried in a hidden tomb, later rediscovered through miraculous means. This tomb, located near the ancient city of Salamis, has become a place of pilgrimage for Cypriots and Christians worldwide, honoring Barnabas as the apostle who first brought the Gospel to the island. Archaeologists excavating in the area have uncovered evidence of an ancient Christian community, including remnants of early Christian worship sites and artifacts that suggest a thriving religious community in Salamis. The association of this site with Barnabas lends historical weight to the belief that his ministry played a foundational role in establishing Christianity on Cyprus.

The most famous story regarding Barnabas's tomb involves its rediscovery in the fifth century, an event recounted by various sources and commemorated in Cypriot tradition. According to the legend, the tomb was located after Barnabas appeared in a dream to a local bishop, revealing its whereabouts. When the tomb was opened, a copy of the Gospel of Matthew was reportedly found resting on his chest. This discovery is said to have strengthened Cyprus's claim to independence in ecclesiastical matters, supporting the Cypriot Church's autonomy from the Patriarchate of Antioch. While archaeological verification of these events remains challenging, the veneration of Barnabas's tomb and the traditions surrounding its discovery highlight his importance in the religious life of Cyprus and the early Church.

In addition to his tomb, ancient churches dedicated to Barnabas have been discovered and studied by archaeologists, particularly in Cyprus and parts of the Mediterranean region where his influence was most pronounced. These churches often contain mosaics, inscriptions, and other artistic representations that reflect the early Christian veneration of Barnabas. In some sites, remnants of frescoes depict Barnabas alongside Paul or in scenes of teaching and healing, suggesting that these communities viewed him as a spiritual father and teacher. The art and architecture of these early churches reveal the significance of Barnabas's ministry in the eyes of the early Christians, whose devotion to him endured for centuries. The presence of churches bearing his name attests to the respect and reverence with which he was regarded by those who sought to honor his legacy.

One notable archaeological find related to Barnabas's influence is a series of inscriptions and early Christian symbols discovered in Cyprus and Asia Minor. These inscriptions, some bearing the Greek name Βαρνάβας (Barnabas), reflect the ways in which early Christian communities recorded their faith and marked sacred spaces. Symbols such as the ichthys (fish), crosses, and simple carvings referencing Christian teachings have been found near sites traditionally associated with Barnabas. These markings serve as silent witnesses to the faith of early Christians, suggesting that Barnabas's teachings and legacy inspired these communities to proclaim their beliefs openly, even in an era of persecution.

Another interesting find is the discovery of early Christian relics believed to have been associated with Barnabas or his ministry. Relics, though sometimes controversial due to the challenges in verifying authenticity, were highly revered in the early Church and often served as focal points for worship and pilgrimage. Among the relics attributed to Barnabas are fragments of the bones and the reputed Gospel of Matthew found with his body, both of which were venerated in Cyprus and were thought to have protective and miraculous qualities. These relics contributed to Barnabas's enduring legacy, drawing pilgrims who sought healing, spiritual strength, or simply the chance to connect with the apostle's memory. The relics, whether authentic or symbolic, reflect the deep reverence for Barnabas in early Christian spirituality and underscore his influence in shaping Christian practice and tradition.

Archaeological studies of the region where Barnabas conducted his missionary work reveal much about the socio-political landscape he navigated, including cities in Cyprus, Asia Minor, and the broader Roman Empire. Excavations of urban centers like Antioch, Iconium, and Salamis have uncovered evidence of complex, multicultural societies where Roman, Hellenistic, and Jewish influences converged. These findings illuminate the context in which Barnabas and Paul carried out their mission, helping historians understand the challenges they faced in spreading a new faith amid established religious and cultural traditions. Artifacts such as Roman coins, pottery, and public inscriptions from these cities illustrate the blend of cultures and beliefs that characterized the communities Barnabas sought to reach, and they offer a window into the world he inhabited.

The architecture of early Christian meeting places, such as house churches and converted buildings, provides insight into how the first Christians, including followers of Barnabas, practiced their faith. Archaeological discoveries in locations associated with Barnabas's journeys show evidence of modest gathering spaces that reflect the simplicity and communal spirit of the early Church. These meeting places, often located in private homes, indicate that Barnabas's early followers valued fellowship and shared worship over grandiose structures. Artifacts found at these sites, such as oil lamps, tableware, and simple crosses, suggest a focus on communal worship, where gatherings were centered around teaching, prayer, and the breaking of bread. These findings align with the values Barnabas is known to have championed—community, humility, and mutual support.

Archaeologists have also uncovered evidence of early Christian burial practices in regions where Barnabas ministered, providing a glimpse into the beliefs and customs of these communities. Christian burial sites from this period often display symbols of resurrection and hope, such as the anchor, fish, and cross, which reflect the early Christians' faith in eternal life. These symbols echo the teachings of Barnabas, who preached a message of salvation, hope, and renewal. The care and reverence evident in these burial practices reflect the influence of apostolic teachings on early Christian communities and suggest that Barnabas's message of faith and resurrection left a lasting impression on his followers.

In addition to these physical artifacts, ancient manuscripts discovered through archaeology have contributed to a greater understanding of Barnabas's influence on early Christian thought. Copies of New Testament texts, including the Acts of the Apostles and the Pauline Epistles, found in monastic libraries and desert caves often contain marginal notes, early commentaries, and annotations that reference Barnabas's teachings or missionary activities. These manuscripts, preserved over centuries, demonstrate the care with which early Christians documented and transmitted the teachings of their faith. The survival of these texts underscores the importance of figures like Barnabas in shaping the beliefs and practices of early Christianity.

Archaeological finds associated with Barnabas provide a tangible link to the early Christian world and to the life of a man whose dedication to spreading the Gospel changed the course of history. Each discovery, whether a relic, an inscription, or an ancient manuscript, serves as a reminder of the enduring power of faith and the ways in which Barnabas's legacy continues to shape Christian thought and devotion. These artifacts and sites, preserved through the centuries, bear witness to the life of a man who left everything to follow Christ and to bring the message of salvation to the world.

As archaeologists continue to explore sites associated with Barnabas and the early Church, new discoveries may further illuminate the mysteries of his life and the profound impact of his ministry. Each artifact, site, and text adds to the rich narrative of Barnabas's life and to our understanding of early Christianity, deepening the appreciation for the faith and perseverance of those first followers who laid the foundations of the Church. Through these archaeological finds, Barnabas's story lives on, inspiring believers to connect with the roots of their faith and to honor the legacy of one of Christianity's earliest apostles.

Chapter 41
Ecological Dimension and Spirituality

In recent decades, scholars and theologians have increasingly examined the ecological dimensions of faith, seeking insight from scriptural teachings, Christian traditions, and the lives of early apostles. Barnabas's life and legacy offer compelling themes for exploring how spirituality and environmental stewardship intersect. Though he lived in a time with a vastly different understanding of ecology, aspects of Barnabas's teachings and approach resonate with modern concerns about care for creation. His actions, humility, and profound respect for community life can be seen as an invitation to reconsider humanity's relationship with the natural world through a Christian lens of respect, stewardship, and interconnectedness.

Throughout his ministry, Barnabas exhibited a deep respect for the interdependent community—a value central to ecological awareness. In his time, communities relied on local resources, and the wellbeing of each person was intricately tied to the health of their environment. As a figure who encouraged unity and compassion, Barnabas's example invites believers to consider how interdependence extends to the natural world. His call for harmony within the early Christian community and his ministry's emphasis on cooperation and support reveal a perspective that transcends the individual, extending to a shared responsibility for God's creation.

Barnabas's teachings and actions reflect an attitude of humility and simplicity that aligns with ecological values of restraint and mindfulness. When Barnabas sold his possessions to support the nascent Church, he exemplified a selfless renunciation of material wealth for the sake of community welfare. This decision speaks to the spiritual virtue of simplicity, a quality increasingly relevant in an era marked by excessive consumption and resource depletion. By choosing to live with less and to focus on the spiritual over the material, Barnabas embodied a lifestyle that aligns with principles of sustainability and conscious resource use. His example challenges modern Christians to consider how their own lifestyles impact the environment and to pursue a life that values the wellbeing of the whole community over individual gain.

Furthermore, Barnabas's missionary journeys highlight his willingness to immerse himself in diverse regions and cultures, a testament to his respect for the people and places he encountered. As he traveled across the Mediterranean—through rural areas, mountains, and bustling cities—Barnabas displayed a deep respect for the uniqueness of each place and the people who called it home. This openness reflects an appreciation for creation's diversity and the beauty of God's world, as well as a recognition that all lands and cultures have a place within God's plan. In this light, Barnabas's life can be seen as an affirmation of the sacredness of all creation, inviting believers to view the earth as God's handiwork and to care for it accordingly.

Barnabas's emphasis on community care and his alignment with the teachings of Jesus also underscore themes of restoration and healing. Many of the stories surrounding Barnabas depict him as a figure of encouragement, someone who uplifted those who were marginalized or struggling. His ministry was defined by acts of kindness and generosity, which can be interpreted as a model for healing relationships not only among people but also between people and the earth. Just as Barnabas encouraged individuals to seek wholeness in their spiritual lives, his example calls Christians to seek wholeness in their relationship with the environment. His life encourages believers to see environmental stewardship as an extension of the Christian mission, a way to live out the call to love and respect all of God's creation.

The ecological implications of Barnabas's legacy also align with the biblical principles of stewardship and dominion, concepts rooted in the creation narratives. Genesis describes humankind's role as stewards of the earth, tasked with caring for and cultivating the world God created. Barnabas's dedication to the Christian community, his generosity, and his willingness to sacrifice for the greater good all mirror this calling to stewardship. His actions reflect a belief that true leadership and dominion mean serving and nurturing rather than exploiting or taking advantage of resources. Barnabas's example challenges modern Christians to adopt a vision of dominion that emphasizes protection, conservation, and reverence for the earth.

In recent years, environmental theologians have highlighted the relevance of figures like Barnabas as models for an eco-spirituality that integrates care for creation into the Christian life. His virtues—compassion, simplicity, and communal responsibility—are particularly suited to an ecological framework. Environmental crises such as climate change, deforestation, and pollution raise questions about ethical stewardship, and Barnabas's example encourages believers to approach these challenges with humility, courage, and a commitment to justice. His legacy invites Christians to consider how their faith calls them to respond to environmental degradation and to take concrete steps to protect the world for future generations.

In some Christian communities, Barnabas has become an informal patron for ecological initiatives, inspiring movements focused on sustainability and conservation. Churches and religious organizations have drawn on his life as a model for community-based environmental action, encouraging practices like sustainable farming, habitat restoration, and community gardening as expressions of Christian stewardship. These efforts, inspired by Barnabas's commitment to community welfare, emphasize the importance of responsible resource use, the preservation of biodiversity, and the care of local environments. In this way, Barnabas's legacy continues to inspire believers to take proactive steps to protect the earth and its resources.

The tradition of pilgrimage to sites associated with Barnabas, such as his tomb in Cyprus, also reflects an ecological dimension of his legacy. Pilgrimage encourages believers to connect with the physical world in a meaningful and reverent way, fostering a sense of connection to the land and to creation itself. The act of pilgrimage reminds Christians that faith is not confined to spiritual realms but is rooted in the physical world—a world that God declared good. This embodied experience of faith reflects an ecological spirituality that honors the material world and emphasizes the interconnectedness of all creation. Pilgrimages to sites associated with Barnabas thus serve as reminders of the importance of honoring and preserving the earth as a sacred gift from God.

Barnabas's influence on Christian thought and community life also underscores the importance of an ethic of care—both for people and the environment. His dedication to supporting and encouraging others reveals a compassionate worldview that can be extended to the care of all creation. Just as Barnabas saw the value in nurturing faith within his community, modern believers are called to nurture and protect the world around them. His example teaches that stewardship extends beyond human relationships to encompass all of God's creatures and the natural systems that sustain life.

In light of Barnabas's legacy, modern Christians are encouraged to consider how environmental stewardship is integral to their faith. His life serves as a reminder that spiritual integrity includes a responsibility to protect the earth and to ensure its beauty and resources endure for future generations. By following Barnabas's example of humility, simplicity, and communal care, believers can cultivate an ecological spirituality that reflects a commitment to justice and reverence for creation.

Finally, Barnabas's teachings about unity and interconnectedness, particularly in his role as a mediator in the early Church, provide a metaphor for humanity's interconnectedness with the environment. Just as Barnabas sought unity among believers, his example encourages Christians to see themselves as part of a larger, interconnected world where the health and wellbeing of one element impacts the whole. This holistic perspective resonates with the ecological understanding that humanity is not separate from nature but deeply integrated within it, dependent on the earth for sustenance, beauty, and life. In honoring this interconnectedness, Barnabas's legacy challenges believers to cultivate a relationship with the environment that is based on respect, protection, and gratitude.

The ecological dimension of Barnabas's legacy invites Christians to adopt an ethic of care that encompasses all aspects of creation. His life encourages a vision of faith that honors the sacredness of the earth, one that seeks to preserve and protect it for future generations. In this way, Barnabas's legacy serves as a call to environmental stewardship, reminding Christians that love of neighbor and love of creation are inseparably linked. Through his example, Barnabas continues to inspire a faith that sees the beauty of God's world as a reflection of divine goodness and invites believers to be faithful stewards of this precious gift.

Chapter 42
Academic Studies and Modern Research

Modern scholarship has approached Barnabas from multiple perspectives, reflecting an academic interest in better understanding his role in the early Church, the social and historical context of his ministry, and his theological influence. Through studies in history, archaeology, theology, and biblical literature, scholars have deepened our understanding of Barnabas, piecing together a complex portrait of his life and contributions. Research on Barnabas not only enriches our knowledge of this early apostle but also sheds light on the broader context of the first Christian communities and the challenges they faced. His life continues to inspire investigation, with each new study contributing to a more nuanced understanding of his legacy and his role in shaping the Christian faith.

One area of academic study has focused on Barnabas's background and cultural identity. Scholars have examined his origins in Cyprus, exploring the implications of his Hellenistic Jewish heritage and how it may have shaped his perspectives and ministry. As a Levite from a Greek-speaking Jewish community, Barnabas was uniquely positioned to act as a bridge between Jewish and Gentile believers, facilitating early Christian expansion into non-Jewish communities. Modern research into the socio-political context of Cyprus during the first century has provided valuable insights into how Barnabas's background influenced his approach to ministry, especially in the multicultural environments he encountered throughout the Roman Empire. This understanding underscores Barnabas's role as a cultural mediator and illuminates how his identity may have informed his inclusive approach to spreading the Gospel.

The Book of Acts is a primary source for scholars studying Barnabas's life, but it has also raised questions due to its selective focus on certain events and figures. While Acts portrays Barnabas as a key leader in the early Church, his prominence diminishes as Paul's mission becomes the central narrative. This shift has led scholars to explore why Barnabas's contributions, though substantial, receive comparatively less emphasis in later chapters. Some researchers suggest that the author of Acts, traditionally identified as Luke, prioritized Paul's mission to the Gentiles, which may have contributed to the relative overshadowing of Barnabas's role. Scholars have examined this dynamic, considering how the literary and theological goals of Acts may have influenced the portrayal of its central figures. By analyzing these narrative choices, modern research seeks to reclaim a fuller picture of Barnabas's role, recognizing his influence on the early Christian movement and his contributions to its theological and missional foundations.

The apocryphal *Epistle of Barnabas* has also been a focal point of modern scholarship, providing insights into early Christian thought and doctrinal development. Though it is unlikely that Barnabas authored this letter, the text has been studied for its distinctive theology, which interprets the Hebrew scriptures through an allegorical lens. This interpretative approach, which presents Jewish customs as symbols foreshadowing Christian truths, has attracted the interest of scholars examining the early Church's complex relationship with its Jewish roots. The *Epistle of Barnabas* offers a window into the theological debates of the time, particularly regarding the transition from Jewish law to Christian grace. Scholars continue to study this epistle as a representative example of early Christian literature, considering how it reflects the Church's evolving identity and its efforts to distinguish itself from traditional Judaism.

Another significant aspect of modern research has focused on Barnabas's involvement in the Council of Jerusalem, as described in Acts 15. The council's decision to accept Gentile converts without requiring adherence to all Jewish laws was a defining moment for the early Church, and Barnabas's advocacy for inclusivity had a lasting impact on Christian theology. Academic studies on the Council of Jerusalem have examined the theological, cultural, and social factors that influenced this decision, emphasizing Barnabas's role in shaping a more inclusive vision of the Christian community. His efforts to bridge Jewish and Gentile believers are seen as foundational to the Church's mission of universal salvation, and scholars have analyzed his contributions to understand how early Christianity developed its unique identity in a diverse and multicultural world.

The historical relationship between Barnabas and Paul has been another area of academic inquiry, especially their separation over a disagreement concerning John Mark. This episode has been analyzed not only as a personal conflict but as an example of how early Christian leaders navigated theological and practical differences. Scholars have explored various dimensions of this event, considering whether it reflects differing leadership styles, theological perspectives, or personal loyalties. This examination has contributed to a more nuanced understanding of early Church dynamics, illustrating the ways in which these leaders managed disagreements while remaining committed to their shared mission. The separation between Barnabas and Paul has also been studied as a precursor to later theological divergences within Christianity, making it a valuable case study for understanding how the early Church accommodated diversity.

Recent archaeological discoveries in Cyprus and other regions where Barnabas ministered have provided further material for academic study. Excavations near Salamis, where Barnabas is believed to have been martyred, have uncovered artifacts and remnants of early Christian communities that may date back to his time. These findings, though limited, offer tangible evidence of Christianity's early presence in the region and support the tradition that Barnabas played a significant role in establishing the faith in Cyprus. Scholars specializing in early Christian archaeology have used these discoveries to piece together a more complete picture of Barnabas's influence, examining how local communities integrated his teachings and practices into their spiritual lives. Through these archaeological studies, researchers gain insight into the daily lives of early Christians and the cultural contexts in which Barnabas's mission unfolded.

In addition to archaeology, textual studies have enriched our understanding of Barnabas's theological legacy. Scholars have explored his portrayal in early Christian writings outside the New Testament, such as the works of Clement of Alexandria and Eusebius of Caesarea, who both regarded Barnabas as a significant apostolic figure. These early Church Fathers viewed Barnabas as a model of faith and as a key figure in the Church's mission to the Gentiles. By studying references to Barnabas in patristic literature, researchers have traced the evolution of his image and influence, analyzing how different Christian communities remembered and honored him. These studies highlight the ways in which Barnabas's legacy was preserved, adapted, and celebrated across diverse Christian traditions, reflecting his enduring importance to the faith.

Modern scholars have also examined the social and economic aspects of Barnabas's ministry, particularly his decision to sell his property to support the early Christian community. This act of generosity has been interpreted as a testament to his commitment to communal life and his rejection of material wealth. Researchers have analyzed this decision in the context of first-century social structures, considering how early Christians navigated issues of wealth, poverty, and communal responsibility. By studying the economic dynamics of the early Church, scholars have gained insight into the social values that Barnabas promoted, particularly his emphasis on solidarity, mutual aid, and the redistribution of resources to support the vulnerable.

The question of Barnabas's influence on later Christian monasticism has also attracted scholarly attention. His emphasis on simplicity, communal life, and generosity inspired early monastic communities, which saw in him a model of ascetic devotion and selflessness. Scholars have traced connections between Barnabas's teachings and the values upheld by early monastic orders, exploring how his legacy influenced the development of Christian asceticism. In examining these connections, researchers have considered how Barnabas's life embodied the principles that would later define monastic spirituality, particularly his focus on humility, community, and service to others.

Finally, Barnabas's legacy has been a subject of interest in ecumenical studies, where scholars explore his role in promoting unity and inclusivity within the early Church. His work in Antioch, his advocacy at the Council of Jerusalem, and his partnership with both Jewish and Gentile believers have been studied as examples of early Christian efforts to build a universal faith community. Researchers in ecumenical theology see Barnabas as a figure who transcended cultural and religious divisions, laying the groundwork for a Church that could embrace diversity without sacrificing unity. This aspect of his legacy has informed contemporary discussions on Christian unity, inspiring those who seek to build bridges between denominations and promote interfaith dialogue.

In recent years, academic studies on Barnabas have expanded to include interdisciplinary approaches, integrating insights from history, theology, sociology, and literary analysis. This multi-faceted approach has allowed scholars to appreciate the complexity of Barnabas's life and the diverse ways in which his legacy has been interpreted and reinterpreted over time. Each study, whether focused on historical context, theological contributions, or social impact, adds depth to our understanding of Barnabas as a pivotal figure in the early Church.

Through these academic pursuits, modern scholarship continues to uncover new dimensions of Barnabas's influence, affirming his role as a foundational figure in Christianity. His life and teachings remain a source of inspiration, both for scholars who seek to understand the early Church and for believers who find guidance in his example. As research advances, the legacy of Barnabas only grows richer, offering insights into the nature of faith, the challenges of leadership, and the enduring call to live lives of compassion, humility, and unity.

Chapter 43
Contemporary Relevance

In an era of rapid change and global challenges, the life and legacy of Barnabas remain strikingly relevant to modern spirituality and Christian practice. His journey as an apostle, his dedication to fostering unity, his resilience in the face of adversity, and his unwavering commitment to faith exemplify qualities that inspire believers today. Barnabas's example offers insights into how Christians can approach their own spiritual lives and engage with the world around them, emphasizing values of inclusivity, encouragement, service, and faithfulness that transcend historical boundaries. His life invites believers to find meaning and direction as they navigate the complexities of contemporary life, fostering a spirituality that is grounded, compassionate, and engaged with the needs of the world.

One of the most significant aspects of Barnabas's contemporary relevance lies in his commitment to unity and inclusivity. In an increasingly divided world, Barnabas's actions remind Christians of the importance of building bridges across cultural, social, and religious divides. His work to include Gentiles in the early Church serves as a timeless example of how faith communities can create spaces that welcome diversity while honoring shared beliefs. Barnabas's legacy challenges modern Christians to foster inclusivity within their own communities, encouraging them to welcome people of different backgrounds and perspectives. His emphasis on unity resonates deeply with today's ecumenical and interfaith efforts, inspiring believers to work toward harmony and mutual understanding with those who may hold different beliefs or traditions.

Barnabas's life also speaks to the value of encouragement, a quality that is as essential now as it was in the early Church. Known as the "son of encouragement," Barnabas uplifted those around him, offering support and belief in their potential even when others doubted them. In an era where many people face anxiety, doubt, and loneliness, Barnabas's example reminds believers of the transformative power of encouragement. His mentorship of figures like Paul and John Mark illustrates the impact that a single act of support can have on another person's life and faith. In contemporary contexts, whether in family, friendship, or community, Barnabas's legacy calls on Christians to be sources of encouragement, helping others to grow, overcome challenges, and deepen their own faith.

Barnabas's dedication to community life and shared resources is another aspect of his relevance to modern believers. His decision to sell his property to support the needs of the Christian community illustrates a profound commitment to social responsibility and care for the common good. This example challenges contemporary Christians to consider how their own resources—time, talents, and possessions—might be used to support those in need. In a world marked by inequality and poverty, Barnabas's generosity serves as a model for fostering communities where resources are shared and the wellbeing of others is prioritized. His life encourages believers to see wealth and material possessions not as ends in themselves but as means of serving others and contributing to the greater good.

The resilience Barnabas demonstrated throughout his ministry offers inspiration to those who face personal or societal challenges. As a missionary, Barnabas encountered opposition, rejection, and physical hardship, yet he remained steadfast in his faith and mission. His resilience, grounded in his love for Christ and his commitment to spreading the Gospel, serves as an example for those facing trials in their own lives. In a time when many experience feelings of isolation, uncertainty, and disillusionment, Barnabas's perseverance reminds believers of the strength that comes from faith and purpose. His example encourages Christians to face adversity with courage, to remain committed to their values, and to trust in God's presence even in difficult circumstances.

In addition, Barnabas's role as a peacemaker is particularly relevant in today's polarized world. His dedication to fostering unity within the early Church, his role in reconciling differing perspectives at the Council of Jerusalem, and his ability to mediate conflicts among believers exemplify qualities that are needed now more than ever. Barnabas's life encourages Christians to be agents of peace in their own communities, promoting understanding and reconciliation where there is division. His example invites believers to approach disagreements with humility and to seek solutions that prioritize harmony and the common good. In a world often divided along ideological and cultural lines, Barnabas's legacy challenges Christians to model the peace of Christ, working to build relationships that reflect mutual respect and compassion.

Barnabas's emphasis on mentorship and guidance speaks directly to the needs of contemporary Christian communities. His support of emerging leaders, especially in his role as a mentor to Paul and John Mark, highlights the importance of nurturing new generations in faith. In modern churches, where leadership and discipleship are crucial to spiritual growth, Barnabas's example provides a model for investing in others and helping them realize their potential. His willingness to guide and encourage others reminds Christians of the value of mentorship, both within the Church and in broader social contexts. Barnabas's legacy calls on believers to foster relationships of trust and to support one another's spiritual journeys, ensuring that future generations are equipped to carry forward the faith.

Moreover, Barnabas's life challenges modern Christians to embrace a mission-oriented spirituality that reaches beyond the walls of the Church. His commitment to spreading the Gospel, even in unfamiliar and sometimes hostile environments, serves as a reminder that faith is not a private endeavor but a calling to share God's love with the world. In a globalized world facing complex issues, from climate change to social injustice, Barnabas's mission-centered approach encourages Christians to engage with the world and to respond to its challenges with compassion and conviction. His legacy calls on believers to embody the Gospel in their actions, using their talents and resources to address the pressing needs of their communities and to make a positive impact on society.

Barnabas's example of humility is also deeply relevant to contemporary spirituality. Though he played a significant role in the early Church, Barnabas remained humble, prioritizing the mission over personal recognition. He worked alongside others, supported emerging leaders, and put the needs of the community above his own. In an age where success is often measured by individual achievement and public acclaim, Barnabas's humility serves as a countercultural reminder that true greatness lies in serving others. His life encourages Christians to approach their own roles with a spirit of humility, valuing cooperation over competition and recognizing that the mission of the Church is a collective endeavor.

Barnabas's respect for diversity within the Christian community also resonates with the modern emphasis on inclusivity. His advocacy for Gentile inclusion reflects a vision of faith that transcends cultural boundaries, welcoming all people into the body of Christ. In a world where cultural, racial, and ethnic diversity are increasingly celebrated, Barnabas's inclusive approach reminds Christians that the Church is called to be a place of welcome for all. His example challenges believers to honor the uniqueness of each person while fostering a community where all are valued and respected. Barnabas's legacy encourages Christians to view diversity not as a source of division but as a reflection of God's creativity and love.

Finally, Barnabas's life serves as a source of inspiration for those who seek to integrate faith with environmental stewardship. His respect for community, simplicity, and shared resources aligns with principles of ecological responsibility, offering a model for a faith that honors creation. In an age where environmental concerns are urgent, Barnabas's example calls Christians to consider how their own actions impact the planet and to adopt lifestyles that reflect a commitment to sustainability. His legacy challenges believers to view care for creation as an integral part of their spiritual lives, a way of honoring God's gift of the earth and ensuring its wellbeing for future generations.

Through his life and legacy, Barnabas provides a timeless example of what it means to live a life of faith in service to others. His qualities—encouragement, humility, resilience, and compassion—continue to speak to the needs of the modern world, offering Christians a model for how to live out the Gospel in their everyday lives. Barnabas's example reminds believers that faith is not just a matter of belief but a way of life, one that calls them to engage with the world, to build inclusive communities, and to respond to challenges with hope and love.

In an era marked by complexity and uncertainty, Barnabas's legacy remains a beacon of hope and inspiration. His life encourages believers to pursue unity, to serve with humility, and to live with a sense of purpose rooted in God's love. Through his example, Barnabas invites Christians to embrace a spirituality that is vibrant, inclusive, and deeply engaged with the world—a spirituality that reflects the values of the early Church and speaks powerfully to the challenges and opportunities of the present day.

Chapter 44
Interfaith Dialogue

Barnabas's life and mission, marked by inclusivity, adaptability, and respect for diverse cultures, provide a powerful framework for interfaith dialogue. As a key figure in the early Church who embraced both Jewish and Gentile believers, Barnabas modeled a faith that could transcend cultural boundaries. His legacy offers insights into how Christians today can approach conversations with people of different religious traditions, engaging in dialogue that fosters mutual understanding and respect. In an increasingly interconnected world, Barnabas's approach serves as a guide for building relationships across faiths, advocating for unity, peace, and collaboration in addressing shared challenges.

One of the most significant aspects of Barnabas's example for interfaith dialogue is his role as a bridge between cultures. As a Levite from Cyprus, Barnabas was rooted in his Jewish faith while also familiar with Hellenistic culture and the customs of the Greco-Roman world. His background uniquely positioned him to engage with people from different religious and cultural traditions, fostering connections that transcended traditional divisions. Barnabas's ability to navigate these diverse environments reminds modern believers of the importance of understanding and respecting the beliefs and customs of others. His life encourages Christians to approach interfaith dialogue with openness, seeing it as an opportunity to build bridges rather than create barriers.

Barnabas's work in Antioch, a vibrant and multicultural city, illustrates his commitment to inclusivity and his willingness to embrace believers from varied backgrounds. Antioch was one of the first places where Jewish and Gentile believers worshiped together, and Barnabas's leadership was instrumental in fostering this unity. His success in Antioch demonstrates how a spirit of hospitality and openness can create communities where people of different faiths and cultures can connect, exchange ideas, and develop mutual respect. For Christians engaged in interfaith dialogue, Barnabas's example underscores the importance of creating spaces where people feel valued and welcomed, allowing for meaningful conversations that honor each person's unique perspective.

In addition to his role as a bridge-builder, Barnabas's humility provides a model for engaging in interfaith conversations with respect and equality. Throughout his ministry, Barnabas demonstrated a commitment to serving others without seeking recognition or asserting dominance. His humility allowed him to work alongside figures like Paul and John Mark, valuing collaboration over personal status. This approach is essential in interfaith dialogue, where humility enables participants to listen actively, to learn from each other, and to recognize the inherent dignity in all people. Barnabas's example encourages Christians to enter into dialogue not as authorities but as equals, fostering a spirit of mutual respect and openness to learning from the experiences and insights of others.

The teachings of Barnabas also emphasize the importance of unity, a theme that resonates deeply in the context of interfaith relations. His advocacy for unity among early Christians, despite cultural and religious differences, reflects his belief in the power of shared values to transcend divisions. In today's diverse religious landscape, this principle of unity can serve as a foundation for interfaith dialogue, encouraging people from different traditions to find common ground. Barnabas's life reminds Christians that while theological differences may exist, there are also shared values—such as compassion, justice, and the desire for peace—that can bring people together. His legacy invites believers to focus on these commonalities, building relationships that strengthen the bonds of humanity and promote a collective vision for a just and peaceful world.

Barnabas's resilience and adaptability also offer valuable lessons for interfaith engagement. His missionary work required him to adapt to new cultures and to communicate the message of the Gospel in ways that resonated with diverse audiences. This flexibility and willingness to meet people where they were reflects an openness that is essential for interfaith dialogue. In conversations with people from different religious backgrounds, adaptability allows Christians to understand others' perspectives, to appreciate the richness of different traditions, and to find ways to communicate their own beliefs respectfully. Barnabas's example encourages believers to approach interfaith dialogue not with rigid expectations but with a willingness to engage in meaningful and evolving conversations.

One of the central values that guided Barnabas's ministry was compassion, a quality that has universal resonance across religious traditions. Barnabas's compassion was evident in his support for marginalized communities, his encouragement of others, and his dedication to building inclusive communities. In interfaith contexts, compassion serves as a common language that can bridge divides and foster understanding. Christians who follow Barnabas's example of compassion can engage in dialogue that prioritizes empathy, understanding, and the wellbeing of others. His legacy encourages believers to approach interfaith interactions with kindness and to seek opportunities for collaboration that promote human dignity and address shared concerns.

Barnabas's relationship with Paul, especially their partnership in ministry, also offers insights into interfaith collaboration. Though they were both Christians, Barnabas and Paul came from different backgrounds and at times held different views. Their ability to work together despite these differences reflects the importance of mutual respect and shared purpose, values that are equally important in interfaith work. For Christians engaging with people of other faiths, Barnabas's relationship with Paul demonstrates how cooperation is possible even when beliefs are not fully aligned. This approach encourages believers to seek partnerships based on shared values, focusing on common goals that benefit society as a whole.

The Council of Jerusalem, where Barnabas advocated for the inclusion of Gentile converts without requiring adherence to all Jewish customs, further exemplifies his commitment to openness and respect for diversity. The decision reached at the council allowed for greater inclusivity within the Christian community, setting a precedent for accepting people from various backgrounds. This inclusivity serves as a model for interfaith dialogue, where openness to diversity is crucial for meaningful engagement. Barnabas's role at the council demonstrates how the Church can navigate cultural and theological differences while remaining faithful to its core mission. For modern Christians, his example invites an approach to interfaith dialogue that is inclusive, flexible, and focused on building relationships based on shared values and respect.

In recent years, Barnabas's legacy has inspired Christian communities involved in interfaith initiatives aimed at addressing global challenges. Issues such as poverty, climate change, and social justice transcend religious boundaries, requiring collaborative efforts from people of all faiths. Barnabas's dedication to community and service aligns with the goals of interfaith initiatives that seek to create a more just and compassionate world. His life encourages Christians to see interfaith work as an extension of their faith, a way to live out the teachings of Christ by working alongside others to improve society. Through collaboration on shared goals, Barnabas's example fosters a vision of faith that is active, inclusive, and deeply engaged with the world.

The relevance of Barnabas's legacy in interfaith dialogue is also reflected in his emphasis on forgiveness and reconciliation. His willingness to reconcile with John Mark after their disagreement demonstrates a commitment to healing relationships and moving beyond past conflicts. In interfaith dialogue, this spirit of reconciliation is essential, as historical tensions and misunderstandings can create barriers to mutual understanding. Barnabas's example encourages Christians to approach interfaith interactions with a willingness to forgive, to let go of past grievances, and to seek genuine connection. His life reminds believers that reconciliation is a path to deeper understanding and unity, allowing people of different faiths to build relationships based on trust and respect.

Barnabas's legacy has inspired various interfaith events and initiatives where his teachings are highlighted as a model for engagement across religious boundaries. Many churches, drawing on his example, have hosted interfaith gatherings, dialogues, and service projects that bring together people from different traditions. These initiatives, which reflect Barnabas's spirit of inclusivity and compassion, offer opportunities for Christians to learn about other faiths, to share their own beliefs, and to work together for the common good. His legacy challenges believers to embrace diversity and to see interfaith work as a way to embody the love of Christ in a world that is both richly varied and deeply interconnected.

Finally, Barnabas's emphasis on hope and encouragement serves as a guiding principle for interfaith dialogue. His unwavering commitment to uplifting others, even in difficult circumstances, reminds Christians of the power of hope in building relationships and fostering understanding. Interfaith dialogue, like any meaningful endeavor, requires patience, resilience, and a commitment to seeing the good in others. Barnabas's example encourages believers to approach interfaith work with optimism, trusting that even small steps toward understanding and unity can make a difference. His legacy inspires Christians to be beacons of hope in a world where divisions often overshadow connections, inviting them to be agents of peace and unity.

Through his life, Barnabas modeled a faith that transcended boundaries, a spirit of openness and respect that remains relevant to the Church's mission today. His legacy invites Christians to engage in interfaith dialogue not as a compromise of their beliefs but as an expression of their commitment to love, respect, and understanding. In a world that is both diverse and deeply connected, Barnabas's example encourages believers to build bridges, to seek common ground, and to work alongside people of all faiths in pursuit of a just, compassionate, and peaceful world. His life serves as a reminder that faith can be a source of unity, and that true discipleship calls believers to engage with all people in the spirit of love and mutual respect.

Chapter 45
Popular Devotion Worldwide

The devotion to Barnabas spans across continents, reflecting his legacy as one of the early apostles who brought the Gospel to diverse peoples. His life, marked by humility, generosity, and a dedication to unity, resonates with believers in many Christian traditions who seek his intercession and guidance. The reverence for Barnabas is evident in churches, shrines, feast days, and folk traditions worldwide, each celebrating his contributions to the Christian faith in ways that reflect local cultures and histories. Through this global devotion, Barnabas's spirit continues to inspire, connecting communities across centuries and reminding them of the enduring power of faith and compassion.

In Cyprus, Barnabas holds a particularly revered place as the island's patron saint. His role as the apostle who first brought Christianity to Cyprus has made him an integral part of the nation's religious identity, and his legacy is woven into the fabric of Cypriot culture. Each year, on June 11, Cypriot Christians celebrate the Feast of Saint Barnabas with services, processions, and gatherings that honor his life and his role as a spiritual protector of the island. Pilgrimages to his reputed tomb near Salamis and the Monastery of Saint Barnabas underscore his importance as both a historical and spiritual figure. These celebrations are marked by a sense of deep reverence, and the people of Cyprus look to Barnabas as a guardian who intercedes on their behalf, protecting their land and guiding them through challenges.

In addition to Cyprus, devotion to Barnabas is widespread across the Mediterranean, reflecting his missionary journeys through regions that include modern-day Turkey, Greece, and Italy. In these areas, churches bearing his name honor his contributions as one of the first apostles who reached out to diverse communities, bridging cultural divides and fostering early Christian unity. For Mediterranean Christians, Barnabas embodies the values of openness and inclusivity that define the early Church, inspiring them to carry forward these qualities in their own lives. His feast day is observed with special liturgies and prayers that celebrate his life and his role in spreading the Gospel across the region, creating a lasting bond between the apostle and the faithful who honor his memory.

In Italy, Barnabas is venerated in a number of churches and regions, especially in places where early Christian history is preserved and celebrated. In Milan, the Basilica di San Barnaba is dedicated to him, and local traditions reflect his importance as a figure of encouragement and charity. Italians who honor Barnabas often see him as a patron of reconciliation, someone whose intercession is sought in times of family or community conflict. Through prayers and devotions, Italian Christians ask for Barnabas's help in fostering peace and understanding, viewing his life as a model for resolving conflicts with humility and compassion. His legacy resonates with their commitment to maintaining harmony within families and communities, and his name is often invoked in prayers for unity and healing.

In the Ethiopian Orthodox Church, Barnabas is remembered as an apostle who played a role in the expansion of Christianity to Africa. Ethiopian Christians celebrate his contributions on various feast days, and his life is often recounted as an example of apostolic courage and devotion. The Ethiopian Church, with its deep ties to early Christian history, sees Barnabas as a part of the ancient tradition that connected the first apostles to believers across continents. His memory is preserved in Ethiopian iconography, hymns, and liturgical readings that emphasize his faith, humility, and dedication to spreading the Gospel. Ethiopian

Christians draw strength from Barnabas's example, celebrating him as a figure whose life exemplified the courage and resilience needed to bring the message of Christ to new lands.

In Latin America, Barnabas is venerated in many communities, where his role as a missionary resonates with believers who draw inspiration from his efforts to reach diverse populations. Devotions to Barnabas often emphasize his compassion and his commitment to uplifting others, qualities that resonate deeply within Latin American spirituality. In countries such as Mexico, Peru, and Brazil, believers often invoke Barnabas as a protector of the poor and a helper in times of hardship. His image, displayed in churches and homes, serves as a reminder of the Gospel's call to care for the vulnerable, and his life encourages believers to practice compassion and charity. Barnabas's feast day is celebrated with masses and prayers that honor his spirit of encouragement, inspiring Latin American Christians to persevere in their faith and to extend compassion to those in need.

In the Philippines, devotion to Barnabas has grown within local Catholic communities, where he is admired as a figure of encouragement and hope. Filipino Christians, who value close-knit family and community relationships, resonate with Barnabas's role as a mentor and supporter within the early Church. His image is sometimes displayed in homes, and his intercession is sought for strength, guidance, and support in family matters. Filipino Catholics celebrate his feast day with prayers and gatherings, asking for his help in maintaining family unity and community harmony. Barnabas's legacy as a "son of encouragement" inspires many in the Philippines to embody his kindness and resilience, especially in times of hardship and loss.

In the United States, Barnabas is honored in various denominations, where he is often recognized as a model of missionary zeal and interfaith dialogue. Many churches dedicated to Barnabas emphasize his role as a peacemaker, reflecting his ability to bridge cultural and religious divides. This aspect of his legacy is particularly resonant in multicultural communities, where his example of inclusivity and understanding inspires Christians to engage with others in a spirit of mutual respect. Barnabas's feast day in the United States is often celebrated with services and community events that emphasize themes of unity, reconciliation, and service, encouraging believers to follow his example in fostering harmony and compassion within their communities.

In Eastern Orthodox communities, Barnabas is venerated with special reverence as an apostle and companion of Saint Paul. Orthodox Christians honor his feast day with liturgical readings and prayers that celebrate his missionary work and his contributions to the early Church. Icons of Barnabas depict him as a steadfast figure, often holding a scroll or a Gospel, symbolizing his role as a teacher and proclaimer of Christ's message. Eastern Orthodox Christians see Barnabas as a figure who embodies the apostolic spirit, and his life inspires them to live out their faith with courage and humility. His legacy in the Orthodox tradition is a reminder of the Church's ancient roots, and believers look to him as a guide for living a life of faithful discipleship.

In Africa, Barnabas is honored as an apostle who contributed to the spread of Christianity across the continent. African Christian communities, particularly those with roots in early Christian traditions, celebrate Barnabas's feast day with songs, prayers, and gatherings that reflect his enduring impact. African believers see in Barnabas a model of faith that is both resilient and adaptable, embodying qualities that resonate deeply within their cultural and spiritual values. His commitment to community life and his emphasis on generosity inspire African Christians to embrace values of hospitality, solidarity, and mutual support. Barnabas's life encourages them to strengthen their own faith communities and to support each other in living out the Gospel.

In the Coptic Orthodox Church of Egypt, Barnabas is revered as an early apostle whose teachings helped shape the foundations of the Christian faith. Coptic Christians celebrate his memory with special prayers, services, and readings from scripture that highlight his missionary efforts and his commitment to unity within the Church. The Coptic devotion to Barnabas emphasizes his role as a figure of encouragement and faith, and his life serves as a reminder of the Church's ancient heritage. Coptic Christians view Barnabas as a protector and intercessor, a figure who connects them to the apostolic age and whose life inspires them to remain steadfast in their faith.

Across these diverse communities, Barnabas's life and legacy continue to inspire devotion, offering believers a model of faith that transcends cultural boundaries. His values of encouragement, compassion, and unity resonate with Christians worldwide, and his example calls them to live lives of service and humility. The global devotion to Barnabas reflects his universal appeal, connecting people of different cultures, languages, and traditions through a shared admiration for his commitment to spreading the Gospel.

Through these practices of popular devotion, Barnabas remains a living presence in the lives of millions, reminding them of the enduring relevance of his message. His life calls believers to embody the virtues he championed, to embrace diversity, and to foster unity within their communities. Barnabas's legacy, celebrated worldwide, is a testament to the power of faith to transcend borders and to bring people together in a spirit of love, compassion, and shared purpose.

Chapter 46
Educational Legacy

Barnabas's influence on the development of Christian educational practices, institutions, and spiritual formation is evident in the numerous schools, seminaries, and programs that honor his name and legacy. Known for his role as a mentor, encourager, and teacher, Barnabas inspired generations of Christians to prioritize education not only for personal growth but also as a means of deepening one's faith and equipping others to spread the Gospel. His dedication to the spiritual formation of early believers has left an indelible mark on the history of Christian education, making him an enduring model for those who view education as a sacred duty and calling.

In the early Church, Barnabas's role as a mentor and guide was foundational in nurturing future leaders, including Paul and John Mark. Barnabas's commitment to these early disciples exemplifies the importance of spiritual mentorship, an educational model that focuses on one-on-one guidance, support, and accountability. This method of teaching, rooted in personal connection, has continued throughout Christian history in the form of discipleship programs, mentorships, and spiritual direction. Christian educators today, following Barnabas's example, emphasize the importance of personal engagement with students and encourage the formation of strong mentor-mentee relationships that foster not only intellectual but also spiritual growth.

The educational legacy of Barnabas is also reflected in the countless seminaries and theological institutions that draw inspiration from his life and teachings. These institutions uphold his dedication to the spread of the Gospel and his commitment to preparing believers to engage with the world thoughtfully and faithfully. Many seminaries and theological schools emphasize the values of humility, resilience, and compassion—qualities that Barnabas embodied in his ministry. By focusing on holistic spiritual development and a balanced approach to theological studies, these institutions continue to cultivate leaders who are grounded in both intellectual and spiritual depth, mirroring Barnabas's approach to ministry.

Barnabas's influence has also shaped Christian curricula that emphasize the development of a compassionate and inclusive worldview. His openness to Gentile converts, his role as a bridge between different cultures, and his dedication to unity inspire educational models that prioritize respect for diversity and the cultivation of empathy. Many Christian educational programs encourage students to view learning as a path toward greater understanding of others, fostering an environment where diversity is celebrated and different perspectives are valued. Following Barnabas's example, these programs aim to develop compassionate leaders who can navigate cultural and social differences with grace, promoting unity within the Christian community and beyond.

The legacy of Barnabas extends to programs that emphasize practical service as an essential component of Christian education. Barnabas's commitment to communal welfare, as seen in his decision to sell his property for the benefit of others, inspires a model of education that integrates service with learning. Many Christian schools and universities encourage students to participate in community service, missions, and outreach projects, reflecting Barnabas's belief that knowledge should be accompanied by action. These programs seek to instill a sense of responsibility and purpose, teaching students that their education is not solely for personal advancement but for the betterment of society and the service of God's kingdom.

In addition to seminaries and service-oriented programs, Barnabas's legacy has influenced Christian educational philosophy itself, particularly in how educators approach character formation. His example of encouragement, generosity, and humility serves as a model for moral and spiritual education, guiding students to develop virtues that are foundational to Christian living. Many schools incorporate Barnabas's values into their curricula, emphasizing the importance of personal integrity, kindness, and a sense of purpose. Through courses in ethics, spiritual formation, and leadership, students are encouraged to adopt these qualities, preparing them to be compassionate and ethical leaders who embody the principles of their faith in their personal and professional lives.

Theological education that draws on Barnabas's example often includes an emphasis on ecumenism and interfaith understanding. Barnabas's legacy of inclusion and his commitment to bridging divides inspire educational approaches that prioritize unity and mutual respect among different Christian traditions. Many Christian colleges and seminaries encourage students to study other denominations and faith traditions, fostering a spirit of openness and dialogue. This approach not only enriches students' understanding of their own faith but also equips them to engage in respectful conversations with people of other beliefs. By learning from Barnabas's inclusivity, educational institutions promote a vision of Christianity that embraces diversity within the faith and fosters peaceful interfaith relations.

Barnabas's focus on mentorship is echoed in the modern emphasis on pastoral education, where future clergy are trained to guide their congregations with wisdom, empathy, and resilience. Pastoral education programs that honor Barnabas's legacy place a strong emphasis on counseling, community building, and spiritual support, preparing ministers to nurture the faith of others as he did. Barnabas's dedication to guiding Paul and John Mark provides a model for pastors, chaplains, and other religious leaders who see their role as that of a mentor, providing guidance and encouragement to those in their care. By focusing on both theological knowledge and interpersonal skills, these programs help create leaders who are equipped to meet the spiritual and emotional needs of their communities.

Christian education inspired by Barnabas's legacy often includes an emphasis on resilience and adaptability. Barnabas's ministry was marked by both success and hardship, and his ability to persevere through challenges offers a valuable lesson for students and educators alike. Many Christian schools and universities encourage students to cultivate resilience, teaching them to approach obstacles with faith and courage. By fostering an environment that values growth through challenge, these institutions prepare students to navigate the complexities of life with a spirit of perseverance, reflecting Barnabas's unwavering commitment to his mission.

In missionary training programs, Barnabas's influence is particularly strong, as his life exemplifies the qualities needed for effective and compassionate ministry. His journeys across diverse regions, his respect for different cultures, and his commitment to spreading the Gospel inspire training programs that emphasize cultural sensitivity, adaptability, and a deep love for humanity. Missionary schools that honor Barnabas's legacy teach students to approach mission work with humility and openness, valuing relationships over conversions and respecting the unique cultures and traditions of the communities they serve. This approach, rooted in Barnabas's example, fosters missionaries who are prepared not only to share the Gospel but to serve as genuine partners and allies in the communities they encounter.

Barnabas's life has also shaped the development of Christian educational literature, particularly in the genre of biographies and hagiographies that highlight his virtues and contributions. Through books, articles, and devotionals, Christian educators and authors share the story of Barnabas with new generations, using his life as a teaching tool to inspire faith and moral integrity. His story is often included in Christian education programs for children and youth, where it serves as a model of courage, compassion, and commitment to God. By including Barnabas's story in educational materials, Christian educators ensure that his legacy continues to shape the spiritual formation of young believers.

Barnabas's legacy also informs contemporary approaches to social justice education within Christian contexts. His commitment to supporting the poor and advocating for inclusivity serves as a foundation for programs that emphasize justice, compassion, and advocacy for marginalized communities. Christian institutions that draw on his example often include courses on social justice, ethical leadership, and community engagement, encouraging students to view their faith as a call to action in service of the greater good. Inspired by Barnabas's generosity and dedication to communal welfare, these programs prepare students to address social inequalities and to promote justice and peace within their communities and beyond.

Finally, Barnabas's educational legacy can be seen in programs that emphasize lifelong learning, encouraging believers to continually grow in faith, knowledge, and wisdom. Barnabas's dedication to teaching and mentorship reflects a belief in the transformative power of education and the importance of ongoing spiritual and intellectual development. Many Christian institutions encourage graduates to view learning as a lifelong journey, one that deepens their understanding of God and strengthens their commitment to serving others. This philosophy, rooted in Barnabas's example, invites believers to pursue growth at every stage of life, nurturing their faith and expanding their understanding in ways that enrich both themselves and their communities.

Through these diverse educational initiatives, Barnabas's legacy as a teacher, mentor, and encourager endures, shaping the values and goals of Christian education around the world. His life calls believers to embrace learning not only as a path to personal growth but as a means of deepening their faith and preparing themselves to serve others. By following Barnabas's example, Christian educators continue to inspire generations to live lives of compassion, resilience, and purpose, ensuring that his legacy remains a vibrant part of the Christian educational tradition.

Chapter 47
The Eternal Legacy of Barnabas

The legacy of Barnabas endures as a testament to the transformative power of faith, compassion, and unwavering dedication. Known as the "Son of Encouragement," Barnabas's life exemplifies a spirituality rooted in humility, service, and a boundless capacity to uplift others. His contributions to the early Church, his mentorship of Paul and John Mark, his courage in the face of adversity, and his dedication to building unity and inclusivity have left an indelible mark on Christian history. Through his actions, Barnabas embodied the essence of a faith that seeks not only to transform the individual but to nurture a community united by love, resilience, and a shared mission.

Barnabas's life calls us to reflect on the role of encouragement in faith. His steadfast support for those around him, even when others doubted them, underscores the impact of a single person's belief in the potential of others. As a mentor to Paul, Barnabas played a pivotal role in shaping one of Christianity's most influential apostles. By giving Paul a second chance and standing by him when others hesitated, Barnabas demonstrated a faith that sees beyond the past, one that looks forward with hope and confidence. His encouragement of John Mark, despite earlier failings, offers a powerful lesson in forgiveness and the redemptive power of second chances. In Barnabas's legacy, we find a call to approach others with understanding and to cultivate relationships that empower people to realize their God-given potential.

Barnabas's life also challenges us to embrace the spirit of unity, especially in a world where division often prevails. His role as a bridge between Jewish and Gentile believers speaks to his commitment to inclusivity and his vision of a Church that transcends cultural and ethnic boundaries. At a time when the Church faced internal disagreements and external challenges, Barnabas worked tirelessly to foster harmony, showing that true strength lies in unity. His legacy invites us to celebrate diversity within the Church, viewing each person's unique background and perspective as a valuable contribution to the whole. Barnabas's example calls believers to reject divisions, to seek understanding, and to honor the shared mission that binds all Christians together.

The generosity of Barnabas, demonstrated in his decision to sell his property to support the early Christian community, reflects a faith that prioritizes communal welfare over personal gain. His actions remind us that true discipleship requires a spirit of selflessness, a willingness to share our resources and to place the needs of others above our own. Barnabas's example is a reminder that faith without action is incomplete; his generosity challenges modern believers to live out their faith in tangible ways, supporting those in need and creating communities that embody the love of Christ. His legacy calls us to consider how we might use our own resources—whether material, spiritual, or emotional—to uplift others and to contribute to a world marked by justice, compassion, and mutual care.

Through his missionary work and his resilience in the face of hardship, Barnabas exemplifies a faith that is active, courageous, and deeply rooted in love for others. His willingness to journey to new lands, to engage with unfamiliar cultures, and to endure the difficulties of ministry reveals a commitment to spreading the Gospel that is unwavering and expansive. Barnabas's resilience in times of adversity, whether in personal conflicts or external challenges, demonstrates that true faith endures not because it is easy, but because it is grounded in an unshakeable trust in God's purpose. His legacy challenges believers to approach their own struggles with courage, to persist in their mission despite setbacks, and to draw strength from the knowledge that they are part of a greater story.

Barnabas's humility serves as a profound reminder that greatness in the Kingdom of God is measured not by status but by service. Though he played a foundational role in the early Church, Barnabas was content to work quietly, lifting others up and placing the mission above personal recognition. His life challenges modern believers to resist the pull of pride and ambition, to approach their own roles with humility, and to remember that the true purpose of leadership is to serve. Barnabas's humility reminds us that the path to greatness is found in acts of kindness, in the quiet encouragement of others, and in a life devoted to God's will.

The devotion to Barnabas across cultures and centuries highlights the universal appeal of his character and the timeless relevance of his teachings. From Cyprus to Africa, from Latin America to Europe, Barnabas is honored as a protector, a healer, a teacher, and an intercessor. His example transcends borders, speaking to believers from all walks of life and reminding them that faith knows no boundaries. The global devotion to Barnabas reflects a shared admiration for his values of encouragement, unity, and service, values that continue to inspire people from diverse backgrounds. His legacy is a testament to the power of faith to bring people together, to foster understanding, and to create communities rooted in love.

Barnabas's life also resonates deeply with those who seek to live out a faith that is ecumenical and inclusive. His commitment to bridging divides within the early Church, his openness to Gentile believers, and his willingness to engage in dialogue with others offer a model for Christians who seek to foster unity across denominations and faith traditions. In a world that is both richly diverse and deeply interconnected, Barnabas's legacy provides a framework for interfaith dialogue, encouraging believers to approach others with respect, humility, and a spirit of collaboration. His life invites Christians to embrace a vision of the Church that is welcoming, compassionate, and committed to building bridges rather than walls.

In an age of environmental concern and social responsibility, Barnabas's legacy calls believers to extend their compassion to all of creation. His respect for community, his sense of shared responsibility, and his commitment to communal welfare align with a vision of faith that honors the earth and cares for the vulnerable. Barnabas's example reminds Christians that stewardship is an integral part of discipleship, that faith is lived out in acts of care for both people and the planet. His legacy encourages believers to view their responsibilities not only in terms of individual actions but as part of a collective mission to preserve God's creation and to ensure its flourishing for future generations.

The story of Barnabas is ultimately a story of love—love for God, love for others, and love for the world. His life embodies the call to be a "son of encouragement," someone who lifts others up, who fosters unity, and who spreads the message of Christ's love to all people. Through his dedication to the Gospel, his generosity, and his unwavering faith, Barnabas invites each of us to live lives that reflect the love of God in all we do. His legacy is a powerful reminder that true discipleship is not defined by doctrine alone, but by a way of being that embodies compassion, humility, and hope.

As we reflect on the life of Barnabas, we are reminded that his story is not just a historical account but a living legacy. His example calls each believer to consider how they, too, might become "sons and daughters of encouragement," people who embody the values he championed and who strive to make the world a place of peace, justice, and unity. In honoring Barnabas's legacy, we are invited to carry forward his mission, to be bearers of hope in a world that longs for healing, and to walk in the footsteps of an apostle who taught us that love is the truest measure of faith.

The eternal legacy of Barnabas is one of inspiration and challenge. His life encourages believers to rise above divisions, to nurture others with kindness, and to remain steadfast in their mission. Through his teachings, his actions, and his unwavering faith, Barnabas leaves behind a legacy that transcends time, inviting each new generation to follow his example and to live lives that reflect the love, courage, and grace that he embodied. As long as there are those who seek to follow Christ with humility, courage, and compassion, the legacy of Barnabas will continue, a testament to the enduring power of faith and the transformative impact of a life lived for others.

Epilogue

Reaching the end of these pages, you have walked a path of questions and reflections that go beyond the traditional account of events surrounding Christ. The figure of Barnabas, who reemerges here as a key witness to a nearly lost chapter of Christianity, reveals a vision of faith and humanity that challenges simplistic dogmas. Throughout his journey, Barnabas was not only a follower or disciple; he was a bridge between worlds, between cultures and perspectives, a fearless spirit in his quest for a deeper understanding of divine purpose. Now, at the conclusion of this work, you are invited to contemplate what it truly means to live out the faith that Barnabas preserved—a faith that, far from being static, moves and adapts, revealing new horizons of spirituality and truth.

The words and teachings found in the Gospel of Barnabas may not be included in official canons, yet they awaken something powerful and timeless: the search for truth. By presenting a narrative that challenges established teachings, it reminds us that faith is not merely about unchanging rites or traditions, but rather an ongoing journey of self-discovery and connection with the divine. Through Barnabas, we encounter a Christ who transcends the limitations of a sanctified image and becomes a reflection of universal truth, a symbol of sacrifice and redemption that resonates across all cultures and times.

This work is not merely a record of historical events; it is an opportunity for you to reflect on the nature of beliefs, on what is sacred, and on what it means to live an authentic spiritual life. If, as Barnabas suggests, there was a divine intervention that spared Jesus from crucifixion, what does that tell us about the role of sacrifice? And if the essence of Christ's message goes beyond suffering and death, where then lies the true power of his life and teachings? These are questions that cannot be answered by reason alone; they require deep reflection, a dive into the layers of one's own faith.

Barnabas teaches us that spiritual authenticity is not defined by titles, authorities, or recognition, but by the genuine commitment to draw near to the divine in its purest forms. His gospel shows us a Barnabas who never sought human approval but lived to give voice to what he believed to be the true message. He reminds us that the spirit of early Christianity was not one of rigid structures, but of a community driven by compassion, inclusivity, and transformation. In a time when faith was persecuted and Christians were marginalized, Barnabas stood as a pillar of strength, an encourager who urged others to stay strong on their paths.

As you finish reading, you now carry the seed of a new understanding, a call to look beyond what is taught and to explore the possibilities of faith with an open mind and heart. If this narrative has challenged some of your beliefs, let it be the beginning of a personal quest—not for ready-made answers, but for a deeper connection with what you hold sacred. For spirituality, as Barnabas teaches us, is more of a path than a destination; it is the ongoing construction of a relationship with the divine mystery, with love, and with a truth that transcends any written word.

Just as Barnabas dared to walk in uncharted territory, reaching out to those others disregarded, may you too have the courage to question and to embrace mystery. The end of these pages is not a final conclusion but an open door to what is yet to be discovered. May the journey of Barnabas, his doubts and certainties, inspire your own journey of faith and understanding, and may you carry forward the spirit of openness, compassion, and the search for truth that infuses this man's story.

Ultimately, Barnabas's legacy is that of an early Christianity, one not confined by rigid structures, but one that seeks the divine ceaselessly in each experience of life. As you leave these pages, may you feel invited to remain in tune with that quest. For, as Barnabas shows us, true faith does not lie in conformism but in the courage to explore, to reflect, and to find within oneself the reflection of the divine.

www.ingramcontent.com/pod-product-compliance
Lightning Source LLC
LaVergne TN
LVHW040046080526
838202LV00045B/3506